Grade 1

Scott Foresman

Fresh Reads

for Fluency and Comprehension

Teacher's Manual

Glenview, Illinois

Boston, Massachusetts

Chandler, Arizona

Upper Saddle River, New Jersey

The Pearson Promise

As the largest educational publishing company in the world, Pearson is committed to providing you with curriculum that not only meets the Common Core State Standards, but also supports your implementation of these standards with your students.

Pearson has aligned the Common Core State Standards to every grade level of *Scott Foresman Reading Street*, our premier educational curriculum. This product provides an alignment of the Common Core State Standards to the Grade 1 assessment items in *Scott Foresman Reading Street Fresh Reads for Fluency and Comprehension*.

We value your partnership highly and look forward to continuing our mission to provide educational materials that fully satisfy your classroom needs.

ISBN 13: 978-0-328-72635-6
ISBN 10:   0-328-72635-4
3 4 5 6 7 8 9 10 V016 21 20 19 18 17 16 15 14 13

Contents

Unit 3 Changes

Unit 4 Treasures

Unit 5 Great Ideas

NOTES TO THE TEACHER

Introduction

Fresh Reads for Fluency and Comprehension is designed to provide differentiated practice in reading comprehension skills and to prepare children to take the Reading/Language Arts section of standardized tests, state tests, or teacher-made tests. The student book includes the weekly differentiated practice tests to strengthen comprehension skills taught in *Scott Foresman Reading Street.* This Teacher's Manual includes the following: (1) notes on how to use the Fresh Read tests, (2) instructions on how to administer and score a fluency test, (3) two charts on which you may record the progress of your children, and (4) annotated copies of all of the Fresh Read tests indicating the correct answer to all questions.

How to Use the Fresh Read Tests

The purpose of the Fresh Read tests is to give weekly differentiated practice in target comprehension skills taught in *Scott Foresman Reading Street.*

This book contains three Fresh Read tests for each week to be used independently from the main selection in *Scott Foresman Reading Street.* The tests consist of a "Fresh Read" leveled passage (or a drawing) and related comprehension items that focus on the target and review comprehension skills of the week but are written to address varying levels of proficiency—Strategic Intervention (SI), On-Level (OL), and Advanced (A). A code at the bottom of each page tells you the level of each test.

You can assess children's proficiency levels using their responses to oral comprehension questions and their work on the comprehension pages in the Reader's and Writer's Notebook. Fresh Read tests can be done independently, or you may choose to work through them with children in small groups, in order to give support and assess children's progress.

Reading passages to children: Drawings are used instead of written passages in Unit R and Unit 1 for SI and OL tests and in Unit 2 for the SI tests. Allow children to look carefully at the pictures before proceeding to the comprehension questions. In all Units, passages should **not** be read aloud to the children. The passages have been written to reflect the phonics principles, high-frequency words, and vocabulary words taught with the main selections in *Reading Street.* In Unit R and Unit 1, all test questions and answer choices are intended to be read aloud to the children for all three levels of the tests, since children may or may not be able to read them. In Unit 2, the test questions and answer choices are to be read aloud to the children only for the SI and OL tests. Based on your knowledge of your class and their reading abilities, you may choose whether or not to read aloud questions and answer choices in Unit 3.

Other ways to use the Fresh Read test pages:

- use the Strategic Intervention pages for whole-class practice with the comprehension skills and/or test-taking skills

- use the Strategic Intervention pages after introducing the target and review comprehension skills but prior to reading the main selection in the student anthology of *Scott Foresman Reading Street* to assess children's readiness to read that selection

- use the On-Level pages as an assessment tool to check children's understanding of the comprehension skills and/or test-taking skills

- use the On-Level pages to check children's need for further practice, reteaching, or more challenging materials

- use the Advanced pages as a substitute for the comprehension pages in the Reader's and Writer's Notebook for children working above grade level

- use any of the pages as preparation for the Unit Benchmark Test

How to Administer and Score a Fluency Test

A fluency test measures a child's reading rate, or the number of words correctly read per minute (wcpm), on grade-level text the child has not seen before. You may want to use a copy of one of the "On-Level" leveled passages from the Fresh Read tests for this purpose. Make a photocopy for yourself of the passage you will give the child. (The pages in this Teacher's Manual have a scale of running numbers beside the passages to make it easier for you to know how many words the child read during the fluency check, while the passages in the student edition do not have the numbers.) Make sure you have put the child's name and the test date at the top of your copy of the passage. Have a watch or clock with a second hand available for timing the reading.

Give the child a copy of the passage for the test. Note: The child should NOT have seen the passage beforehand; it is a "fresh" reading passage for the child. Do NOT allow the child to read the passage silently before oral reading.

Have the child read the text aloud. Do not have the child read the title as part of the fluency reading; it is not included in the running word count. (You may want to tape-record the child's reading for later evaluation.) Stop the child at exactly one minute and note precisely where the child stopped.

As the child reads orally, on your copy of the text mark any miscues or errors the child makes during the reading (see the chart on page viii). Count the total number of words the child read in one minute. Subtract any words the child read incorrectly. Record the words correct per minute score on the test.

The formula is: Total # of words read – # of errors = words correct per minute (wcpm).

You will likely want to keep the test in your folder for the child. You may also want to record children's progress on the Reading Fluency Progress Chart on page xi and/or the Individual Fluency Progress Chart on page xii.

How to Identify Reading Miscues/Errors

Using the passage on page ix, the chart below shows the kinds of miscues and errors to look for as a child reads aloud and the notations to use to mark them.

Reading Miscue	Notations
Omission The child omits words or word parts.	Then kids go (back) home.
Substitution The child substitutes words or parts of words for the words in the text.	*little* ~~Small~~ kids ride sleds.
Insertion The child inserts words or parts of words that are not in the text.	*can* They ⌄ skate on ponds.
Mispronunciation/Misreading The child pronounces or reads a word incorrectly.	*sled* They can slide down big, slick hills.
Hesitation The child hesitates over a word and the teacher provides the word.	*H* Big kids <u>smile</u>.
Self-correction The child reads a word incorrectly but then corrects the error.	(sc) They can skate on the thick ice.

Notes

- If the child hesitates over a word, wait several seconds before telling the child what the word is.

- If a child makes the same error more than once, count it as only one error.

- Self-correction is not counted as an actual error. However, writing "SC" over the word or words will help you identify words that give the child some difficulty.

Fresh Reads for Fluency and Comprehension

Sample Fluency Test

Here is the passage marked as shown on the previous page. This is the "On-Level" passage from Grade 1, Unit 3, Week 1. As the child reads the passage aloud to you, mark miscues and errors. Have the child read for exactly one minute, and then mark the last word the child reads.

Name *Susan*   9/4/2009   ⑷₂   **A Place to Play**

It Is Cold!

Kids like to play in the cold. Big kids skate. They can skate	13
on thick ice. They ˄*can* skate on ponds. Big kids <u>smile</u>. *(SC)* *H*	23
little ~~Small~~ kids ride sleds They can slide down big, slick hills. *sled*	34
Sleds go fast! Small kids grin.	40
Then kids go ⟨back⟩ home. It is / time to take a hot bath. Then	54
it is time to take a nap!	61

$$47 - 5 = 42$$

Total number of words read   47
Number of errors   − 5
Words correct per minute   42

Interpreting the Results

According to published norms for oral reading fluency, children at the end of Grade 1 should be reading fluently at 60 words correct per minute in text that is on grade level. This chart gives recommended progress toward that goal.

End of Unit/Grade			Reading Rate (wcpm)
Grade 1	Unit R		inappropriate
Grade 1	Unit 1		inappropriate
Grade 1	Unit 2		inappropriate
Grade 1	Unit 3	Weeks 1-3	20 to 30
		Weeks 4-6	25 to 35
Grade 1	Unit 4	Weeks 1-3	30 to 40
		Weeks 4-6	35 to 45
Grade 1	Unit 5	Weeks 1-3	40 to 52
		Weeks 4-6	45 to 60
End of Year Goal			60

If a child's reading rate is lower than the suggested progress toward the standard for his or her grade level, your notes on the child's miscues may help you determine why the rate is low. Does the child make errors that indicate his or her decoding skills are poor? If so, further instruction in phonics may be needed. Do the errors reflect a lack of comprehension or limited vocabulary? In that case, instruction in comprehension strategies and exposure to more vocabulary words may help. A lack of fluency may indicate a lack of exposure to models of fluent oral reading. It may also mean that the child isn't reading enough material at his or her reading level. Encourage the child to read more books or children's magazine articles at an accessible or comfortable level of reading for him or her.

Fresh Reads for Fluency and Comprehension

Reading Fluency Progress Chart

Child's Name	Unit 1		Unit 2		Unit 3		Unit 4		Unit 5	
	Date	WCPM	Date	WCPM	Date	WCPM	Date	WCPM	Date	WCPM
1.										
2.										
3.										
4.										
5.										
6.										
7.										
8.										
9.										
10.										
11.										
12.										
13.										
14.										
15.										
16.										
17.										
18.										
19.										
20.										
21.										
22.										
23.										
24.										
25.										
26.										
27.										
28.										
29.										
30.										
31.										
32.										
33.										
34.										
35.										

Individual Fluency Progress Chart, Grade 1

Name _____

WCPM (vertical axis): 125, 120, 115, 110, 105, 100, 95, 90, 85, 80, 75, 70, 65, 60, 55, 50, 45, 40, 35, 30

Timed Reading/Week (horizontal axis): 1, 2, 3, 4, 5, 6, 7, 8, 9, 10, 11, 12, 13, 14, 15, 16, 17, 18, 19, 20, 21, 22, 23, 24, 25, 26, 27, 28, 29, 30, 31, 32, 33, 34, 35, 36

Fresh Reads for Fluency and Comprehension

Name _____

Look at the pictures. Then answer the questions that follow.

The First Day

Turn the page.

- -

Answer the questions below.

1 How did the boy feel *before* he got on the bus?

● scared
○ happy
○ sleepy

2 How did the boy's mother feel at the *beginning* of the story?

○ angry
○ happy
● worried

3 Where was the boy going?

○ to a park
● to school
○ home

4 Draw or write about how the boy felt *after* he got off the bus.

Answers may vary. Possible response: happy/drawing of a happy face

Common Core State Standards

Questions 1–4: Literature 1. Ask and answer questions about key details in a text. **Literature 3.** Describe characters, settings, and major events in a story, using key details. **Literature 7.** Use illustrations and details in a story to describe its characters, setting, or events.

Fresh Reads   Unit R Week 1 SI

Name _____

Look at the pictures. Then answer the questions that follow.

Pam Skates

1

2

3

4

Turn the page.

Answer the questions below.

1 **How did Pam feel in picture 1?**

○ scared

● happy

○ angry

2 **What did Pam like to do?**

● skate

○ jump rope

○ draw

3 **Where was Pam in picture 3?**

○ park

○ school

● house

4 **What did Pam's mother do?**

○ She went skating.

● She helped Pam.

○ She read a book.

5 **In picture 2, how can you tell that Pam was sad?**

Possible response: She cried.

Common Core State Standards

Questions 1–5: Literature 1. Ask and answer questions about key details in a text. **Literature 3.** Describe characters, settings, and major events in a story, using key details. **Literature 7.** Use illustrations and details in a story to describe its characters, setting, or events.

Name _____

Read the selection. Then answer the questions that follow.

Sam's Books

I see the books. One is green. One is yellow. Two are blue.	13
I like the little green one. I go for the green one. I have my	28
little green book with me.	33
Mom comes to me. We are on a mat. She looks at the green	47
one with me.	50

Turn the page.

Fresh Reads   Unit R Week 1 A

Answer the questions below.

1 **Where is Sam?**

○ in a car

● on a mat

○ in a box

2 **What does Sam like to do?**

● look at a book

○ sleep

○ brush his teeth

3 **Who is with Sam?**

○ a baby

○ Dad

● Mom

4 **Which book does Sam like?**

Possible response: He likes the green book.

5 **How does Mom feel?**

Possible response: She feels happy reading with Sam.

Common Core State Standards

Questions 1–5: **Literature 1.** Ask and answer questions about key details in a text. **Literature 3.** Describe characters, settings, and major events in a story, using key details.

Name _____

Look at the pictures. Then answer the questions that follow.

What Fun!

Turn the page.

Answer the questions below.

1 **Where was the girl in the *first* picture?**

- ○ in a pool
- ○ at the beach
- ● in a park

2 **What did the girl like to do?**

- ● play
- ○ read
- ○ sleep

3 **When did the story take place?**

- ○ in the fall
- ● in the summer
- ○ in the winter

4 **Where was the girl in the *last* picture?**

Possible response: She was at the beach.

Common Core State Standards

Questions 1–4: Literature 1. Ask and answer questions about key details in a text. **Literature 3.** Describe characters, settings, and major events in a story, using key details. **Literature 7.** Use illustrations and details in a story to describe its characters, setting, or events.

Name _____

Look at the pictures. Then answer the questions that follow.

Mat's Day

1

2

3

4

Turn the page.

Answer the questions below.

1 **Where was Mat in the *first* picture?**

○ on a bus

○ in the yard

● in the kitchen

2 **Where was Mat in the *second* picture?**

○ on a bus

● at school

○ in a park

3 **What did Mat like to do in the park?**

● ride his bike

○ run on a path

○ sit on a bench

4 **Where was Mat in the *last* picture?**

○ in his classroom

● in his bedroom

○ in a car

5 **Where was Mat in the *first* and *last* pictures?**

Possible response: He was
at home.

Questions 1–5: **Literature 1.** Ask and answer questions about key details in a text. **Literature 3.** Describe characters, settings, and major events in a story, using key details. **Literature 7.** Use illustrations and details in a story to describe its characters, setting, or events.

Common Core State Standards

Name _____

Read the selection. Then answer the questions that follow.

Where Are You, Pat?

Mom said, "Where are you, Pat?"	6
"On a plane with Sam," said Pat.	13
She said, "Where are you, Pat?"	19
"In a car with Pam," said Pat.	26
She said, "Where are you, Pat?"	32
"On a bus with Nan," said Pat.	39
She said, "Come out of the tub, Pat. I can see you. Come	52
here with me. We have to go."	59

Turn the page.

Answer the questions below.

1 Where did Pat say she was *first*?

- ○ on a bus
- ○ in a bed
- ● on a plane

2 Where did Pat say she was *second*?

- ● in a car
- ○ on a boat
- ○ in bed

3 How did Pat feel in this story?

- ○ She was mad.
- ● She was happy.
- ○ She was sleepy.

4 Where did Pat say she was *last*?

Possible response: She said she was on a bus.

5 Where was Pat all the time?

Possible response: She was in the tub.

Common Core State Standards

Questions 1–5: Literature 1. Ask and answer questions about key details in a text. **Literature 3.** Describe characters, settings, and major events in a story, using key details.

Name _____

Look at the pictures. Then answer the questions that follow.

Getting Ready

1

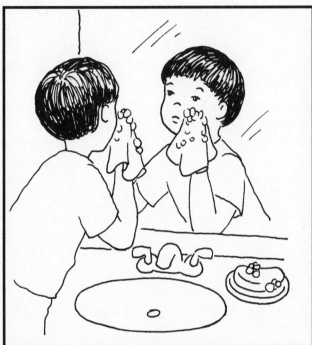

2

3

Turn the page.

Answer the questions below.

1 **What was the *first* thing the boy used?**

○ a comb

● a wash cloth

○ a toothbrush

2 **What did the boy use *next*?**

● a toothbrush

○ a bar of soap

○ a comb

3 **Where was the boy?**

○ He was in his bedroom.

● He was in the bathroom.

○ He was in the kitchen.

4 **What did the boy do *last*?**

Possible response: The boy combed his hair.

Common Core State Standards

Questions 1–4: Literature 1. Ask and answer questions about key details in a text. **Literature 3.** Describe characters, settings, and major events in a story, using key details. **Literature 7.** Use illustrations and details in a story to describe its characters, setting, or events.

Name _____

Look at the pictures. Then answer the questions that follow.

Dinner Time

1

2

3

4

Turn the page.

Answer the questions below.

1 **What did the mom do at the *beginning* of the story?**

○ Mom ate a meal.

● Mom cut a carrot.

○ Mom set the table.

2 **What did the mom do *next*?**

○ Mom read a book.

○ Mom cleaned the table.

● Mom cooked a meal.

3 **What did the boy do in the *third* picture?**

● The boy set the table.

○ The boy ate a meal.

○ The boy cooked a meal.

4 **Where did this story take place?**

○ at a store

● at home

○ at school

5 **What did the family do *last*?**

Possible response: They ate a meal.

Common Core State Standards

Questions 1–5: **Literature 1.** Ask and answer questions about key details in a text. **Literature 3.** Describe characters, settings, and major events in a story, using key details. **Literature 7.** Use illustrations and details in a story to describe its characters, setting, or events.

Name _____

Read the selection. Then answer the questions that follow.

Leaves

Dad, Biff, and Tim go in the car. They go to look at leaves.	14
Tim said, "I see green ones. I see yellow ones."	24
Tim can see yellow leaves on the ground. "Look! Here are	35
big ones. We can fit three in a bag."	44
At home Tim pins up yellow ones. Tim said, "Come see!	55
We have big yellow ones."	60
They come to see. Biff looks. He said, "I like big yellow	72
ones."	73
They said, "We like that."	78

Turn the page.

Answer the questions below.

1 **What happened at the *beginning* of the story?**

○ Tim was in bed.

● The family was in a car.

○ Dad got leaves.

2 **What happened in the *middle* of the story?**

● Tim saw leaves on the ground.

○ Dad got in the car.

○ Biff came to see the leaves.

3 **What did Tim take home?**

● yellow leaves

○ red leaves

○ green leaves

4 **What happened *last* in the story?**

Answers may vary. Possible response: They like the leaves.

5 **Where was Tim at the *end* of the story?**

Possible response: Tim was at home.

Common Core State Standards

Questions 1–5: Literature 1. Ask and answer questions about key details in a text. Literature 3. Describe characters, settings, and major events in a story, using key details.

Name _____

Look at the pictures. Then answer the questions that follow.

Play Date

Turn the page.

Fresh Reads   Unit R Week 4 SI

Answer the questions below.

1 **What did the boy and the frog do at the *beginning* of the story?**

- ○ They rode trikes.
- ● They played with cars.
- ○ They jumped in a pond.

2 **What told you this story was make-believe?**

- ● The frog has on clothes.
- ○ The boy has on clothes.
- ○ The boy rode a trike.

3 **What could *not* really happen?**

- ○ A frog can not jump.
- ○ A boy can not play.
- ● A frog can not ride a trike.

4 **What could really happen in this story?**

Answers may vary. Possible responses: A boy can play with cars. A boy can ride a bike. A frog can jump. A boy can wear clothes.

Common Core State Standards

Questions 1–4: Literature 1. Ask and answer questions about key details in a text. **Literature 3.** Describe characters, settings, and major events in a story, using key details. **Literature 7.** Use illustrations and details in a story to describe its characters, setting, or events. **Literature 9.** Compare and contrast the adventures and experiences of characters in stories.

Name _____

Look at the pictures. Then answer the questions that follow.

What a Night!

1

2

3

4

Turn the page.

Answer the questions below.

1 **What happened at the *beginning* of the story?**

○ The girl read a book.

○ The girl drove a car.

● The girl flew on a bed.

2 **What can really happen?**

○ A girl can be on a cloud.

● A girl can sleep in a bed.

○ A girl can fly a car.

3 **What *can not* be real?**

● a book with a face

○ a bed in a room

○ a girl in a bed

4 **Where can a bed really be?**

○ flying in the air

○ resting on a cloud

● sitting in a room

5 **How can you tell this story is make-believe?**

Possible responses: The girl flies on a bed. The girl flies a car. The book has a face.

1 Copyright © Pearson Education, Inc., or its affiliates. All Rights Reserved.

Common Core State Standards

Questions 1–5: **Literature 1.** Ask and answer questions about key details in a text. **Literature 3.** Describe characters, settings, and major events in a story, using key details. **Literature 7.** Use illustrations and details in a story to describe its characters, setting, or events. **Literature 9.** Compare and contrast the adventures and experiences of characters in stories.

Name _____

Read the selection. Then answer the questions that follow.

The Frog and the Cat

"What can we do?" said the yellow frog.	8
"We can go to see the blue dog," said the green cat.	20
"Not me," said the yellow frog.	26
"Can we look at the big books?" said the green cat.	37
"We can!" said the yellow frog.	43
They look at four books. They like the two blue ones.	54
They hop on the bed. They have fun.	62

Turn the page.

Answer the questions below.

1 Only a make-believe frog can

- ○ be green.
- ● talk with a cat.
- ○ sit in water.

2 What *can not* really happen?

- ○ A frog hops high.
- ○ A cat sees a frog.
- ● A frog likes blue books.

3 What happens at the *end* of the story?

- ● The frog and the cat hop on the bed.
- ○ The frog plays with the dog.
- ○ The frog asks the cat questions.

4 What can really happen?

Answers may vary. Possible response: Cats can be on beds.

5 How can you tell this is make-believe?

Possible response: Cats and frogs can not talk.

Common Core State Standards

Questions 1–5: **Literature 1.** Ask and answer questions about key details in a text. **Literature 3.** Describe characters, settings, and major events in a story, using key details. **Literature 9.** Compare and contrast the adventures and experiences of characters in stories.

Name _____

Look at the pictures. Then answer the questions that follow.

Jill Has Fun

1

2

3

Turn the page.

Answer the questions below.

1 **What happened at the *beginning* of the story?**

○ Jill jumped rope.

● Jill went down a slide.

○ Jill rested in a hammock.

2 **What happened in the *middle* of the story?**

○ Jill played on a swing.

○ Jill played with a dog.

● Jill played with a ball.

3 **What could *not* really happen?**

● Jill is bigger than her house.

○ Jill climbs a ladder.

○ Jill plays with a ball.

4 **What happened at the *end* of the story?**

Possible response: Jill read a book.

Common Core State Standards

Questions 1–4: Literature 1. Ask and answer questions about key details in a text. **Literature 3.** Describe characters, settings, and major events in a story, using key details. **Literature 7.** Use illustrations and details in a story to describe its characters, setting, or events.

Name _____

Look at the pictures. Then answer the questions that follow.

Rain and Sun

1

2

3

4

Turn the page.

Answer the questions below.

1 **How does the story *begin*?**

○ The boys go out.

● The boys talk.

○ The boys play.

2 **In the *middle* of the story, the boys want to**

● play with a ball.

○ go home.

○ look at frogs.

3 **What would make this story make-believe?**

○ The boys are friends.

○ The ball gets wet.

● The sun talks.

4 **In the *middle* of the story, why can't the boys play?**

● It is raining.

○ The sun is out.

○ They do not have a ball.

5 **How does the story *end*?**

Possible response: The boys play ball.

Common Core State Standards

Questions 1–5: Literature 1. Ask and answer questions about key details in a text. **Literature 3.** Describe characters, settings, and major events in a story, using key details. **Literature 7.** Use illustrations and details in a story to describe its characters, setting, or events.

Name _____

Read the selection. Then answer the questions that follow.

The New School

Dan is at a new school. He wants to have a pal. He likes to	15
jog with a pal. He likes to hop with a pal.	26
One day, Sam comes to the school. He has a red cap. He is	40
new like Dan. Dan can see Sam on the yellow bus. He can sit	54
with Sam. Dan likes Sam.	59
Dan and Sam are pals. They are at the top of a hill. They	73
hit a ball with a bat. They let the ball hit a can.	86

Turn the page.

Answer the questions below.

1 **What happens at the *beginning* of the story?**

- ○ Dan plays a little ball.
- ● Dan is at a new school.
- ○ Dan is on a big hill.

2 **What does Dan like to do with a pal?**

- ● jog
- ○ read
- ○ win

3 **How do you know this story could really happen?**

- ○ Dan can fly home.
- ○ Dan is a tan cat.
- ● Dan is at a school.

4 **What does Dan do *after* he sees Sam?**

Possible response: Dan sits
with Sam on the bus.

5 **What happens at the *end* of the story?**

Possible response: Dan and
Sam play ball.

Common Core State Standards

Questions 1–5: Literature 1. Ask and answer questions about key details in a text. Literature 3. Describe characters, settings, and major events in a story, using key details.

Name _____

Look at the picture. Then answer the questions that follow.

The Picnic

Turn the page.

- -

Answer the questions below.

1 **What *can not* really happen?**

○ Bears eat some food.

● Bears read a paper.

○ Bears have a family.

2 **Only a make-believe bear can**

○ have paws.

○ see a tree.

● wear a hat.

3 **Where were the bears?**

○ in a school

● in a park

○ in a house

4 **How can you tell this story is make-believe?**

Answers may vary. Possible responses: The bears are dressed in clothes. The father bear has glasses. The father bear reads.

Common Core State Standards

Questions 1–4: **Literature 1.** Ask and answer questions about key details in a text. **Literature 3.** Describe characters, settings, and major events in a story, using key details. **Literature 7.** Use illustrations and details in a story to describe its characters, setting, or events.

Name _____

Look at the pictures. Then answer the questions that follow.

School Days

Turn the page.

Answer the questions below.

1 **Where *are* the animals?**

● in school

○ on a bus

○ at home

2 **What can really happen?**

○ A dog goes to school.

● A cat takes a nap.

○ A cow jumps a rope.

3 **What *can not* really happen?**

○ A school has toys.

○ A teacher reads books.

● A cat goes to school.

4 **A real school does *not* have**

○ books.

○ balls.

● cows.

5 **How can you tell this story is make-believe?**

Possible responses: The animals wear clothes. The animals go to school.

Common Core State Standards

Questions 1–5: **Literature 1.** Ask and answer questions about key details in a text. **Literature 3.** Describe characters, settings, and major events in a story, using key details. **Literature 7.** Use illustrations and details in a story to describe its characters, setting, or events.

Name _____

Read the selection. Then answer the questions that follow.

The Cat and the Pig

Jen is a little cat. Sid is a big pig. Jen and Sid went to a red | 17

mat. | 18

The mat said, "Nap on me!" | 24

Sid sat on the red mat. He said, "You are little. I can not | 38

nap on you." | 41

Jen sat on the mat. Jen said, "Look! I fit on the red mat. I | 56

can nap on it." | 60

Sid flew to a blue mat. It said, "Nap on me!" | 71

Sid sat on the blue mat. He said, "I fit on the blue mat! I | 86

can nap on it." | 90

Turn the page.

Answer the questions below.

1 What *can not* really happen?

○ A mat can be blue.

○ A pig can look.

● A cat can talk.

2 Where does Sid nap?

○ on a red mat

● on a blue mat

○ on a green mat

3 What can a real pig do?

○ fly

○ talk

● nap

4 What in this story can really happen?

Possible response: A cat can nap on a mat.

5 How can you tell this story is make-believe?

Possible response: A cat and a pig can not talk.

Common Core State Standards

Questions 1–5: Literature 1. Ask and answer questions about key details in a text. **Literature 3.** Describe characters, settings, and major events in a story, using key details. **Literature 9.** Compare and contrast the adventures and experiences of characters in stories.

Name _____

Look at the pictures. Then answer the questions that follow.

Jason Learns to Ride

Turn the page.

Answer the questions below.

1 **What did Jason do *first*?**

○ He rode his bike.

● He put on his helmet.

○ He got help from Mom.

2 **How did Jason feel *before* he rode his bike?**

○ happy

○ sleepy

● scared

3 **How did Jason feel *after* he rode his bike?**

● happy

○ sad

○ angry

4 **How does Jason feel about riding a bike?**

Possible response: He enjoys riding his bike.

Common Core State Standards

Questions 1–4: **Literature 1.** Ask and answer questions about key details in a text. **Literature 3.** Describe characters, settings, and major events in a story, using key details. **Literature 7.** Use illustrations and details in a story to describe its characters, setting, or events.

Name _____

Look at the pictures. Then answer the questions that follow.

The Playful Girl

1

2

3

Turn the page.

Answer the questions below.

1 What did the girl do *first*?

- ○ She watched the rain.
- ● She played ball.
- ○ She rode her bike.

2 What does the girl like to do?

- ● She likes to play.
- ○ She likes to sit.
- ○ She likes to read.

3 How does the girl feel when she plays?

- ○ sad
- ● happy
- ○ tired

4 How does the girl feel when it rains?

- ○ happy
- ○ sleepy
- ● sad

5 What does the girl like doing outside?

Possible responses: The girl likes to play ball. The girl likes to ride her bike.

Common Core State Standards

Questions 1–5: **Literature 1.** Ask and answer questions about key details in a text. **Literature 3.** Describe characters, settings, and major events in a story, using key details. **Literature 7.** Use illustrations and details in a story to describe its characters, setting, or events.

Name _____

Read the selection. Then answer the questions that follow.

Dan's Cat

Dan has a little cat. The cat is Rags. Dad is mad at Rags.   14

Rags gets in Dad's bag. Dad can see Dan and Rags. Dan and   27

Rags have fun in the hot sun. Then, Rags naps on Dan's lap.   40

Dan pats Rags on the back. Rags is happy. Dan likes to have   53

Rags as a pal.   57

Turn the page.

Answer the questions below.

1 **Why is Dad mad?**

○ Rags hurt Dad.

● Rags gets in Dad's bag.

○ Rags is lost.

2 **How does Dan feel about Rags?**

○ mad

○ sad

● glad

3 **What does Rags do just *after* Rags and Dan have fun in the sun?**

● Rags takes a nap.

○ Rags gets in Dad's bag.

○ Rags jumps in a box.

4 **What does Dan do for Rags?**

Possible response: Dan cares for Rags.

5 **How does Rags feel about Dan?**

Rags likes Dan.

Common Core State Standards

Questions 1–5: **Literature 1.** Ask and answer questions about key details in a text. **Literature 3.** Describe characters, settings, and major events in a story, using key details.

Name _____

Look at the pictures. Then answer the questions that follow.

The Lion and the Monkey

Turn the page.

Fresh Reads   Unit 1 Week 2 SI

Answer the questions below.

1 **What happened *first* in the story?**

- ● The lion grew hungry.
- ○ The lion met the monkey.
- ○ The lion ate some food.

2 **The monkey was**

- ● kind to the lion.
- ○ mean to the lion.
- ○ afraid of the lion.

3 **What happened right *after* the lion met the monkey?**

- ○ The monkey grew hungry.
- ○ The monkey ran away from him.
- ● The monkey told him to come.

4 **What happened *last* in the story?**

Possible response: The lion and the monkey had lunch together.

Common Core State Standards

Questions 1–4: Literature 1. Ask and answer questions about key details in a text. **Literature 3.** Describe characters, settings, and major events in a story, using key details. **Literature 7.** Use illustrations and details in a story to describe its characters, setting, or events.

Name _____

Look at the pictures. Then answer the questions that follow.

Fun at the Beach

1

2

3

4

Turn the page.

Answer the questions below.

1 **How does the mouse feel?**

- ● happy
- ○ sad
- ○ mad

2 **What happens *first* in the story?**

- ○ The mouse digs in the sand.
- ● The frog jumps on the beach.
- ○ The pig reads a book.

3 **What happens in the *middle* of this story?**

- ○ The frog jumps on the beach.
- ● The mouse digs in the sand.
- ○ The fox has a picnic lunch.

4 **What happens right *before* the fox has lunch?**

- ● The pig reads.
- ○ The frog jumps.
- ○ The mouse digs.

5 **What happens *last* in the story?**

The fox has a picnic lunch.

Common Core State Standards

Questions 1–5: **Literature 1.** Ask and answer questions about key details in a text. **Literature 3.** Describe characters, settings, and major events in a story, using key details. **Literature 7.** Use illustrations and details in a story to describe its characters, setting, or events.

Fresh Reads   Unit 1 Week 2 OL

Name _____

Read the selection. Then answer the questions that follow.

Max on a Trip

Dear Ken,	2
I was on a trip with my cat, Sam. I had on my big hat. I had	19
a pack on my back.	24
Sam had on a cap. It was tan.	32
We saw Tim. Tim was a big green pig.	41
Tim said, "Come and play tag with me!" We did. We had	53
fun in the sun. Sam and I ran up a hill. Tim said, "I will tag	69
you, Sam." He did.	73
Next we had a fig and a nap.	81
In the end, Sam and I went home.	89
From,	90
Max	91

Turn the page.

Answer the questions below.

1 **What did Max do at the *beginning* of the trip?**

- ● got on a hat
- ○ had a nap
- ○ played tag

2 **Max is**

- ○ mean.
- ● silly.
- ○ sad.

3 **What happened *after* Sam and Max met Tim?**

- ● They played tag.
- ○ They saw a pig.
- ○ They went on a trip.

4 **What did Max do right *after* he had a fig?**

Possible response: He and Sam had a nap.

5 **What did Max do *after* his trip?**

Possible response: He wrote the letter to Ken.

Common Core State Standards

Questions 1–5: **Literature 1.** Ask and answer questions about key details in a text. **Literature 3.** Describe characters, settings, and major events in a story, using key details.

Fresh Reads   Unit 1 Week 2 A

Name _____

Look at the pictures. Then answer the questions that follow.

Ling Plays Ball

Turn the page.

Answer the questions below.

1 **Ling likes to**

● play t-ball.

○ take walks.

○ cook.

2 **Where does this story take place?**

○ at Ling's home

● at a park

○ at a store

3 **How did Ling feel when she hit the ball?**

○ sad

○ angry

● happy

4 **How can you tell this story could really happen?**

Answers may vary. Possible response: A girl could play t-ball.

Common Core State Standards

Questions 1–4: **Literature 1.** Ask and answer questions about key details in a text. **Literature 3.** Describe characters, settings, and major events in a story, using key details. **Literature 7.** Use illustrations and details in a story to describe its characters, setting, or events.

Name _____

Look at the picture. Then answer the questions that follow.

On a Trip

Turn the page.

- -

Answer the questions below.

1 **The boy and the dog are**

● friendly.

○ mean.

○ mad.

2 **How can you tell this story is make-believe?**

○ The boy has a pet dog.

● The boy and the dog are in space.

○ There are stars.

3 **How does the boy feel?**

● happy

○ angry

○ scared

4 **Where does this story happen?**

○ in a park

○ at a school

● in space

5 **How does Zam feel when he sees the boy and dog?**

Possible response: He is glad
to see them.

Common Core State Standards

Questions 1–5: Literature 1. Ask and answer questions about key details in a text. Literature 3. Describe characters, settings, and major events in a story, using key details. Literature 7. Use illustrations and details in a story to describe its characters, setting, or events. Literature 9. Compare and contrast the adventures and experiences of characters in stories.

Name _____

Read the selection. Then answer the questions that follow.

Fox's Box

Fox got in the big box at the pond. It was fun. But the box	15
fell in. It did not stop. Fox got mad. He did not like to get wet.	31
He did not like the box. It was not fun. He had to get back to	47
land.	48
"Help!" Fox said.	51
"Come here!" said Rob.	55
"Where are you?" said Fox.	60
"I am here. Hop in!" said Rob. "You can do it! Come with	73
me!"	74
Fox did it, and he got back.	81

Turn the page.

Answer the questions below.

1 **Where was Fox?**

- ○ on a hill
- ● at a pond
- ○ at his house

2 **How did Fox feel when the box fell in the pond?**

- ○ silly
- ○ happy
- ● mad

3 **Rob liked to**

- ● help.
- ○ run.
- ○ sit.

4 **How did Fox feel at the *end* of the story?**

Possible response: Fox was happy.

5 **How did you know this story was make-believe?**

Possible response: Foxes can not talk.

Common Core State Standards

Questions 1–5: **Literature 1.** Ask and answer questions about key details in a text. **Literature 3.** Describe characters, settings, and major events in a story, using key details.

Name _____

Look at the pictures. Then answer the questions that follow.

The Family

1

2

3

4

Turn the page.

Answer the questions below.

1 **What is the story *mostly* about?**

● a new baby

○ food

○ grandparents

2 **What would be another good title for this story?**

○ A Big House

● Baby Comes Home

○ Time for Bed

3 **What does the family do at the *end* of the story?**

● play with the baby

○ play with toys

○ play outside

4 **Why do you think the family looks tired at breakfast?**

Possible response: The baby cried at night and kept them awake.

1 Copyright © Pearson Education, Inc., or its affiliates. All Rights Reserved.

Common Core State Standards

Questions 1–4: Informational Text 1. Ask and answer questions about key details in a text. **Informational Text 2.** Identify the main topic and retell key details of a text.

Name _____

Look at the pictures. Then answer the questions that follow.

The Builders

Turn the page.

Answer the questions below.

1 **Who do these pictures tell about?**

○ a girl

○ a family

● a girl and a boy

2 **What is this story *mostly* about?**

● A boy and a girl build with blocks.

○ A girl helps.

○ A boy makes something.

3 **The boy and girl**

● work together.

○ play ball.

○ read to each other.

4 **What is another good title for this story?**

○ A Block

● A Tall Building

○ A Little Boy

5 **What happens at the *end* of the story?**

Possible response: The boy and girl make a building.

Common Core State Standards

Questions 1–5: Informational Text 1. Ask and answer questions about key details in a text. **Informational Text 2.** Identify the main topic and retell key details of a text.

Name _____

Read the selection. Then answer the questions that follow.

Bob's Job

Bob gets back from town. He has to get dinner for his	12
animals. He likes to do it. He takes seeds to them.	23
"Eat this up! It will help you get big!"	32
The animals like to eat. Lots of little birds come to eat. Bob	45
likes to look. He sees five yellow ones. He sees two blue ones.	58
Bob likes his job. It is fun.	65

Turn the page.

Answer the questions below.

1 **What was this story _mostly_ about?**

○ playing in the yard

○ getting big and strong

● feeding animals and watching birds

2 **What is another good title for this story?**

○ Yellow Birds

● Bob and the Animals

○ Birds Fly Away

3 **Why did lots of little birds come?**

● They came to eat.

○ They wanted to play.

○ They were hot.

4 **Why did Bob have seeds?**

Possible response: He was feeding his animals.

5 **What happened at the _end_ of the story?**

Possible response: Bob had fun looking at the birds.

Common Core State Standards

Questions 1–5: **Informational Text 1.** Ask and answer questions about key details in a text. **Informational Text 2.** Identify the main topic and retell key details of a text.

Name _____

Look at the pictures. Then answer the questions that follow.

Camping

Turn the page.

Answer the questions below.

1 **Where did this story take place?**

○ in a city

○ in a house

● in a forest

2 **What was this story *mostly* about?**

● camping

○ gardening

○ jumping

3 **What was the *middle* picture all about?**

○ riding to the woods

● setting up the camp

○ having fun after dark

4 **When did the story *end*?**

Possible response: It ended at night.

Common Core State Standards

Questions 1–4: Literature 1. Ask and answer questions about key details in a text. **Literature 3.** Describe characters, settings, and major events in a story, using key details. **Literature 7.** Use illustrations and details in a story to describe its characters, setting, or events.

Name _____

Look at the picture. Then answer the questions that follow.

Jack and the Beanstalk

Turn the page.

Answer the questions below.

1 **What is this story _all_ about?**

⬤ when Jack climbs a beanstalk

◯ what Jack feeds a goose

◯ how Jack builds a castle

2 **The giant is**

◯ a young boy.

⬤ a big man.

◯ an old woman.

3 **What does the giant have in his hand?**

⬤ an egg

◯ a goose

◯ a beanstalk

4 **How does Jack feel when he sees the giant?**

◯ happy

◯ angry

⬤ scared

5 **What tells you that the story happens in the sky?**

Possible response: There are

clouds.

Common Core State Standards

Questions 1–5: Literature 1. Ask and answer questions about key details in a text. **Literature 3.** Describe characters, settings, and major events in a story, using key details. **Literature 7.** Use illustrations and details in a story to describe its characters, setting, or events.

Name _____

Read the selection. Then answer the questions that follow.

Kim's Dinner

Kim and her pals eat dinner on the grass. They see a cat, a	14
pig, and a fox.	18
Kim said, "Can you hum a song, Cat?"	26
"Yes!" said Cat. And he did.	32
"Can you hop on one leg, Pig?" said Kim.	41
"Yes!" said Pig. And he did.	47
"Can you do tricks, Fox?" Kim said.	54
"Yes!" said Fox. And he did.	60
They had fun.	63

Turn the page.

Answer the questions below.

1 **Who can hum a song?**

- ◯ Kim
- ● Cat
- ◯ Fox

2 **Where did Kim have dinner?**

- ● on the grass
- ◯ at school
- ◯ in the park

3 **What was this story *mostly* about?**

- ◯ Kim and her pals read a story.
- ◯ Kim and her pals had a race.
- ● Kim and her pals had fun.

4 **What did Pig do?**

Pig hopped on one leg.

5 **What did Fox do?**

Fox did tricks.

Common Core State Standards

Questions 1–5: Literature 1. Ask and answer questions about key details in a text. **Literature 3.** Describe characters, settings, and major events in a story, using key details.

Name _____

Look at the pictures. Then answer the questions that follow.

Dad and Anna Go Shopping

1

2

3

4

Turn the page.

Answer the questions below.

1 **What did Anna want in picture 1?**

● to eat

○ to sleep

○ to play

2 **Why did Dad and Anna go shopping?**

● They needed food.

○ They had dropped their eggs.

○ They were bored.

3 **Why did Dad and Anna clean the floor?**

○ They went shopping.

○ Dad spilled milk.

● Anna dropped an egg.

4 **Why did Anna drop an egg?**

Possible response: The cat
jumped on her.

Common Core State Standards

Questions 1–4: Informational Text 1. Ask and answer questions about key details in a text. **Informational Text 3.** Describe the connection between two individuals, events, ideas, or pieces of information in a text.

Name _____

Look at the pictures. Then answer the questions that follow.

In the Garden

Turn the page.

Answer the questions below.

1 **What grew in the dirt?**

○ the sun

○ some water

● a plant

2 **Why did the girl and her mom dig a hole?**

● They were planting a bush.

○ They were making mud pies.

○ They were hiding a box.

3 **Why did the girl water the plant?**

○ to make it go away

● to help it grow

○ to clean it

4 **Why did the girl and her mom wear gloves?**

● to keep their hands safe

○ to stay warm

○ to look nice

5 **Why was the girl happy at the *end* of the story?**

Possible response: She was happy because her plant grew and got flowers.

Common Core State Standards

Questions 1–5: Informational Text 1. Ask and answer questions about key details in a text. **Informational Text 3.** Describe the connection between two individuals, events, ideas, or pieces of information in a text.

Name _____

Read the selection. Then answer the questions that follow.

Ron

Ron is sick. He will not go to class. He is at home with	14
Dad. He will not go to bed for a nap. He can look at an animal	30
book for fun. It has a hippo, an elephant, and a zebra. Next	43
Ron plays with his cat. But Ron must rest. Then Ron will get	56
well.	57

Turn the page.

Answer the questions below.

1 **Why was Ron at home?**

- ○ It was raining.
- ● He was sick.
- ○ It was summer.

2 **Why did Ron read a book?**

- ○ He liked zoos.
- ○ He had homework.
- ● He was not tired.

3 **Who did Ron play with?**

- ● his cat
- ○ his dad
- ○ his mom

4 **Why did Ron have to rest?**

Possible response: Ron had to rest to get well.

5 **When will Ron feel better?**

Possible response: Ron will feel better after he rests.

1 Copyright © Pearson Education, Inc., or its affiliates. All Rights Reserved.

Common Core State Standards

Questions 1–5: **Informational Text 1.** Ask and answer questions about key details in a text. **Informational Text 3.** Describe the connection between two individuals, events, ideas, or pieces of information in a text.

Name _____

Look at the pictures. Then answer the questions that follow.

Mr. Cat and Miss Bunny

Turn the page.

Answer the questions below.

1 **What happened *first* in the story?**

- ○ Bunny ate cookies with Cat.
- ● Bunny came to Cat's house.
- ○ Bunny went home for a nap.

2 **What happened *second* in the story?**

- ○ Cat waved at Bunny.
- ○ Cat poured milk.
- ● Cat opened the door.

3 **What happened *last* in the story?**

- ● Cat and Bunny had a snack.
- ○ Cat and Bunny played a game.
- ○ Cat and Bunny said hello.

4 **Why did Bunny come to Cat's house?**

Answers may vary. Possible response: She came to have a snack.

Common Core State Standards

Questions 1–4: Literature 1. Ask and answer questions about key details in a text. **Literature 3.** Describe characters, settings, and major events in a story, using key details. **Literature 7.** Use illustrations and details in a story to describe its characters, setting, or events.

Name _____

Read the selection. Then answer the questions that follow.

Fox Has Fun

Fox likes to jog. She jogs to town. Then she jogs to the	13
park. As she jogs, she sees bugs. She sees ducks, too. Next,	25
she sees the sun. Then Fox jogs home. At home, she sees Dad.	38
She tells him what she saw. She tells him she had lots of fun.	52
She tells Dad to jog with her. Dad will!	61

Turn the page.

Answer the questions below.

1 **Why did Fox jog to town?**

- ● to have fun
- ○ to see Dad
- ○ to get home

2 **Where did Fox jog *first*?**

- ○ to the park
- ○ to her house
- ● to the town

3 **What did Fox see *first*?**

- ○ the ducks
- ● the bugs
- ○ the sun

4 **What did Fox see right *after* she saw ducks?**

- ○ the park
- ○ the bugs
- ● the sun

5 **What did Fox do *last*?**

Possible response: She tells Dad to jog with her.

Common Core State Standards

Questions 1–5: **Literature 1.** Ask and answer questions about key details in a text. **Literature 3.** Describe characters, settings, and major events in a story, using key details.

Name _____

Read the selection. Then answer the questions that follow.

Look, Look, Look!

Fred said, "I want to play ball. Sam and Pam, do you want | 13

to play ball with me?" | 18

"Yes!" said Sam and Pam. | 23

Fred asked, "Do you have a ball?" | 30

They did not have a ball. They all went looking for a ball. | 43

They went looking at home. They went looking in the park. | 54

Then Fred saw his dog Zip. Zip had a ball with him! Then | 67

Fred, Sam, Pam, and Zip had fun playing ball in the park. | 79

Turn the page.

Answer the questions below.

1 **What happened *first* in the story?**

○ Fred wanted to find Zip.

● Fred wanted to play ball.

○ Fred wanted to see the park.

2 **What did Fred ask Sam and Pam *first*?**

○ to get a ball

● to play with him

○ to look for his dog

3 **Where did they look *after* they looked at home?**

● in the park

○ at the school

○ on the bed

4 **Why did they go looking at home?**

Possible response: They wanted to find a ball.

5 **What happened *last* in the story?**

Possible response: They had fun playing ball in the park.

Common Core State Standards

Questions 1–5: **Literature 1.** Ask and answer questions about key details in a text. **Literature 3.** Describe characters, settings, and major events in a story, using key details.

78

Fresh Reads   Unit 2 Week 1 A

Name _____

Look at the pictures. Then answer the questions that follow.

Jane's Juice

1

2

3

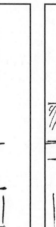

4

Turn the page.

Answer the questions below.

1 Where does Jane drink juice?

- ● at her home
- ○ at her school
- ○ at a park

2 What happens when Jane drinks her juice?

- ○ She gets thirsty.
- ○ She gives juice to her brother.
- ● She starts to cool off.

3 Why does Jane spill her juice?

- ○ The boy opened the door.
- ● The ball bumped Jane's glass.
- ○ The boy bumped into Jane.

4 Why does Jane drink juice?

Possible response: She drinks juice because she is hot from playing ball.

Common Core State Standards

Questions 1–4: Literature 1. Ask and answer questions about key details in a text. **Literature 3.** Describe characters, settings, and major events in a story, using key details. **Literature 7.** Use illustrations and details in a story to describe its characters, setting, or events.

Name _____

Read the selection. Then answer the questions that follow.

What Mom Makes

Sam is six! Mom wants to make a little cake for him. She	13
must mix it up. Then she bakes the cake. It is yellow. Sam	26
likes yellow. Sam's pals come to his home. Mom gets the cake	38
for them. They sit and eat it. It is good! Mom could have made	52
a big cake!	55

Turn the page.

Answer the questions below.

1 **How did Sam feel about his cake?**

○ sad

○ mad

● happy

2 **Why did Mom make the cake?**

● Sam was six.

○ It was her big day.

○ She wanted to eat cake.

3 **Why did Sam's pals come to his home?**

● to eat cake

○ to see Mom

○ to bake a cake

4 **Why did Mom make a yellow cake?**

○ Mom likes yellow.

● Sam likes yellow.

○ Sam's pals like yellow.

5 **Why could Mom have made a big cake?**

Possible response: Sam and his pals ate all of the little cake.

Common Core State Standards

Questions 1–5: **Literature 1.** Ask and answer questions about key details in a text. **Literature 3.** Describe characters, settings, and major events in a story, using key details.

Name _____

Read the selection. Then answer the questions that follow.

Nate Gets to Play

Nate plays in the park with his mom. He runs and he	13
jumps. He plays in the sand. He makes animals with the sand.	25
Then the rain falls, and Nate must go home. At home Nate	37
puts on dry socks. Then he takes a nap. Nate wakes up and	51
sees that the sun is back. Nate smiles. He gets up and walks	64
back to the park with his mom. He is glad that the sun shines.	70

Turn the page.

Answer the questions below.

1 Why did Nate go to the park?
- ● to have fun
- ○ to see the rain
- ○ to take a nap

2 Why did Nate go home?
- ○ It was too hot.
- ○ He was sick.
- ● The rain fell.

3 What did Nate do *after* he put on dry socks?
- ○ He played in the sand.
- ● He took a nap.
- ○ He went home.

4 Why did Nate put on dry socks?

Possible response: His feet were wet.

5 Why did Nate smile at the *end* of the story?

Possible response: He was happy that he could go back to the park.

Common Core State Standards

Questions 1–5: Literature 1. Ask and answer questions about key details in a text. Literature 3. Describe characters, settings, and major events in a story, using key details.

Fresh Reads Unit 2 Week 2 A

Name _____

Look at the pictures. Then answer the questions that follow.

Bike Safety

This is NOT safe.

This is safe.

Turn the page.

Answer the questions below.

1 **The author wanted you to**

○ know about the girl's family.

○ learn how to ride a bike.

● stay safe while riding a bike.

2 **Why did the author write this?**

○ to make you laugh

● to teach you something

○ to tell a make-believe story

3 **Which sentence tells about the pictures?**

● The girl needs to be careful.

○ The girl likes to run.

○ The bike is new.

4 **Why do you think the author used two pictures of the girl?**

Possible response: The author wanted to show the right way and wrong way to ride a bike.

Common Core State Standards

Questions 1–4: **Informational Text 1.** Ask and answer questions about key details in a text. **Informational Text 2.** Identify the main topic and retell key details of a text. **Informational Text 7.** Use the illustrations and details in a text to describe its key ideas.

Name _____

Read the selection. Then answer the questions that follow.

We See Animals

We can see animals in many places. I have a cat at home.	13
A red bird has a nest in my back tree. Animals live at the	27
animal park too. We see the little whales that live there. We see	40
hippos in the pond. At home or at the animal park, we can see	54
many animals.	56

Turn the page.

Answer the questions below.

1 The author wants you to

○ look at many little red birds.

○ see many tall green trees.

● see that animals live in many places.

2 Why does the author write about his cat?

● It is one animal he sees.

○ It is the pet he likes most.

○ He does not have a dog.

3 What does the author like *best*?

○ homes

● animals

○ parks

4 The author does *not* try to

○ tell about hippos.

○ talk about the animal park.

● make you sad.

5 What is this story *mostly* about?

Possible response: It is about where animals live.

Common Core State Standards

Questions 1–5: Informational Text 1. Ask and answer questions about key details in a text. **Informational Text 2.** Identify the main topic and retell key details of a text.

Fresh Reads   Unit 2 Week 3 OL

Name _____

Read the selection. Then answer the questions that follow.

I Like My Neighborhood

I am a big cat. I am glad I live on Pine Drive. My	14
neighborhood has nice people. The man in the yellow house	24
feeds me. The mail people stop to pet me. Miss Smith puts out	37
milk for me. The milk is good. The mice are not too busy to	51
chase me. The birds sing to me all the time. My neighborhood	63
is the best place!	67

Turn the page.

Answer the questions below.

1 Why did the author write this story?

● to make you smile

○ to make you cry

○ to make you mad

2 Who told this story?

○ the birds

● the cat

○ the mice

3 Why did the author write about milk?

○ The author does not like milk.

● The cat likes milk.

○ There is no water.

4 What was this story *mostly* about?

Possible response: It is about the neighborhood of a cat.

5 How did the author make this story funny?

Possible response: The mice run after the cat.

Common Core State Standards

Questions 1–3, 5: Literature 1. Ask and answer questions about key details in a text. Literature 3. Describe characters, settings, and major events in a story, using key details. Question 4: Literature 2. Retell stories, including key details, and demonstrate understanding of their central message or lesson.

90

Fresh Reads   Unit 2 Week 3 A

1 Copyright © Pearson Education, Inc., or its affiliates. All Rights Reserved.

Name _____

Look at the pictures. Then answer the questions that follow.

Jack Needs a Snack

1

2

3

4

Turn the page.

Fresh Reads   Unit 2 Week 4 SI

Answer the questions below.

1 Why did Jack make a sandwich?

○ His dad told him to make one.

● He was hungry.

○ He wanted to feed the cat.

2 What happened *first* in the story?

○ Jack poured some milk.

○ Jack ate a sandwich.

● Jack read a book.

3 What happened *second* in the story?

● Jack made a sandwich.

○ Jack left the kitchen.

○ Jack drank some milk.

4 What was the *last* thing that happened in the story?

Possible response: Jack played with the cat.

Common Core State Standards

Questions 1–3: Literature 1. Ask and answer questions about key details in a text. **Literature 3.** Describe characters, settings, and major events in a story, using key details. **Question 4: Literature 2.** Retell stories, including key details, and demonstrate understanding of their central message or lesson.

Name _____

Read the selection. Then answer the questions that follow.

Nice People

Kim came into my class late in the fall. No one said much | 13
to her. Then at lunch Jan sat with Kim. Kim was glad. Jan | 26
gave grapes to Kim. Kim gave cake to Jan. Then they were | 38
pals. | 39

When Jeff came to class, Kim was nice to him. She said, | 51
"We can all sit together at lunch." | 58

Turn the page.

Answer the questions below.

1 **Why did Jan give grapes to Kim?**

● She wanted to be nice to Kim.

○ She had too many grapes.

○ She wanted to eat cake.

2 **What happened *first*?**

○ Jeff came to class.

○ Jan spoke to Kim.

● Kim came to class.

3 **What happened *after* the girls had lunch?**

○ Kim sat down with Jan.

● They got to be good friends.

○ Jan went to a new school.

4 **What happened *last*?**

○ Kim sat with Jan.

● Kim spoke to Jeff.

○ Jeff came to class.

5 **What happened *after* Jan gave Kim grapes?**

Possible response: Kim gave

cake to Jan.

Common Core State Standards

Questions 1–4: Literature 1. Ask and answer questions about key details in a text. **Literature 3.** Describe characters, settings, and major events in a story, using key details. **Question 5: Literature 2.** Retell stories, including key details, and demonstrate understanding of their central message or lesson.

Name _____

Read the selection. Then answer the questions that follow.

My Cake for Bill

My name is Jill. My twin is Bill. We are now six! I want to | 15

make a cake for Bill. I mix it up. I put it into a pan. Then Mom | 32

and I bake the cake. We put yellow frosting on it. I put six | 46

candles on the cake. Mom lit them. We sing to Bill. He claps | 59

his hands. Then he puffs and puffs but he can not make the | 72

candles go out. They are trick candles. What fun! | 82

Turn the page.

Answer the questions below.

1 The *first* thing Jill did to the cake was

- ○ bake it.
- ● mix it.
- ○ put it in a pan.

2 *After* Jill put frosting on the cake, she

- ● put candles on it.
- ○ clapped her hands.
- ○ helped Bill.

3 What did Bill do *last*?

- ○ clap
- ○ bake
- ● blow

4 Why did Mom and Jill sing to Bill?

Possible response: It was Bill's birthday.

5 What could Bill do *next*?

Answers may vary. Possible response: He could eat cake.

Common Core State Standards

Questions 1–3: Literature 1. Ask and answer questions about key details in a text. **Literature 3.** Describe characters, settings, and major events in a story, using key details. **Questions 4–5: Literature 2.** Retell stories, including key details, and demonstrate understanding of their central message or lesson.

Fresh Reads   Unit 2 Week 4 A

Name _____

Look at the picture. Then answer the questions that follow.

The Silly Race

Turn the page.

Answer the questions below.

1 **Why does Jan Todd have her name on the book?**

○ She ran the race.

● She wrote the story.

○ She was the mouse.

2 **Why do you think the author wrote *The Silly Race?***

○ to teach you about races

○ to tell you about pets

● to make you laugh

3 **Why are there make-believe animals in the book?**

● to make the story funny

○ to tell how to win a race

○ to show how animals live

4 **Why is Mouse smiling?**

Possible response: Mouse smiles because he won the race.

Common Core State Standards

Questions 1–4: Literature 1. Ask and answer questions about key details in a text. **Literature 7.** Use illustrations and details in a story to describe its characters, setting, or events.

Name _____

Read the selection. Then answer the questions that follow.

My Brave Mom

My mom has a good job. Her job is to put out fires. She | 14

puts on a big black hat with a wide brim for her job. She | 28

drives a red truck. She helps people in the neighborhood. She | 39

is brave. I am glad when she comes home safe. When I grow | 52

up, I want to put out fires too. | 60

Turn the page.

Answer the questions below.

1 **Why does the author want to put out fires?**

● He wants to be like his mom.

○ He likes to put on black hats.

○ He wants to ride in red trucks.

2 **Why did the author write this story?**

○ to tell about a red truck

● to tell about his mom

○ to tell about his neighborhood

3 **Why does Mom put on a hat?**

○ to get help

○ to look good

● to be safe

4 **Why did the author tell about Mom's hat?**

○ to tell when it will rain

○ to tell where she lives

● to tell what she looks like

5 **Why does the author think his mom is brave?**

Possible response: Her job is
to put out fires.

1 Copyright © Pearson Education, Inc., or its affiliates. All Rights Reserved.

Common Core State Standards

Questions 1–5: Informational Text 1. Ask and answer questions about key details in a text. **Informational Text 2.** Identify the main topic and retell key details of a text. **Informational Text 8.** Identify the reasons an author gives to support points in a text.

Name _____

Read the selection. Then answer the questions that follow.

A New Pal

Dear Kip,   2

    I have a new pal. He just came to this neighborhood. He   14

lives down the block from me. His name is Jack. He is fun.   27

He is nice too. Jack likes to play ball. He can hit the ball far.   42

He likes to run races. He can run fast. We play together all the   56

time. We have a good time. I am glad I met him.   68

                  Still your good pal,   72

                  Rick   73

Turn the page.

Answer the questions below.

1 **Why is the name of this story "A New Pal"?**

● It is about Jack.

○ It is about a race.

○ It is about a ball.

2 **The author wants Rick's letter to seem**

○ sad.

● real.

○ silly.

3 **Which of these tells how Rick feels about Jack?**

○ His name is Jack.

○ He can run fast.

● I am glad I met him.

4 **Why does Rick like Jack?**

Possible response: Jack is fun to be with.

5 **How can you tell Rick and Kip are pals?**

Possible response: Rick wrote a letter to Kip about a new pal.

Common Core State Standards

Questions 1–5: **Literature 1.** Ask and answer questions about key details in a text. **Literature 3.** Describe characters, settings, and major events in a story, using key details.

Name _____

Look at the pictures. Then answer the questions that follow.

Seasons

Turn the page.

Answer the questions below.

1 **What is the same in each picture?**

● the lamps

○ the weather outside

○ the snow

2 **The author wants you to**

○ learn how birds fly.

○ feel sad when it rains.

● see how the weather changes.

3 **Which things are in all three pictures?**

● the boy, the bed, the lamps

○ the bed, the snow, the curtains

○ the boy, the rain, the lamps

4 **What is different in all the pictures?**

Possible response: The weather outside is different.

Common Core State Standards

Questions 1–4: Informational Text 2. Identify the main topic and retell key details of a text. **Informational Text 3.** Describe the connection between two individuals, events, ideas, or pieces of information in a text. **Informational Text 7.** Use the illustrations and details in a text to describe its key ideas.

Name _____

Read the selection. Then answer the questions that follow.

A Family

A family can be big or small. Dan has a family with a | 13

mom, dad, and nine children. Ann lives with just her mom. | 24

Tom lives with his dad. Ben lives with his mom and his dad. | 37

Max has a family that lives together in a big neighborhood. | 48

Pete has family in many places. A family can come in many | 60

shapes and sizes! | 63

Turn the page.

Answer the questions below.

1 Who has a big family?

○ Ann
● Dan
○ Tom

2 Who has a small family?

● Ann
○ Dan
○ Pete

3 Why does the author say that a family can be big or small?

○ to show how families are the same
● to show how families are different
○ to show different kinds of houses

4 How is Max's family *not* like Pete's family?

○ Max's family works hard.
○ Max's family has a son.
● Max's family lives together.

5 How are Ann's family and Tom's family the same?

Possible response: They both
are small.

Common Core State Standards

Questions 1–5: Informational Text 2. Identify the main topic and retell key details of a text. **Informational Text 3.** Describe the connection between two individuals, events, ideas, or pieces of information in a text.

Fresh Reads   Unit 2 Week 6 OL

Name _____

Read the selection. Then answer the questions that follow.

Two Rabbits

Two rabbits left the pet shop to live with a new family. | 12

Honey was a tan rabbit. She could live inside. Flower was a | 24

white rabbit. He lived outside in a cage. Honey wanted to eat | 36

carrots and hay. Flower wanted to eat hay and rabbit food. | 47

Honey and Flower liked to hop around their new homes. | 57

Honey and Flower had little noses. They were nice rabbits. | 67

Turn the page.

Answer the questions below.

1 **The author wrote this story to tell you about**

○ a new family.

○ all animals.

● two rabbits.

2 **How are Honey and Flower the same?**

○ They are tan.

● They live with a family.

○ They are white.

3 **How is Honey *not* like Flower?**

● Honey lives inside.

○ Honey is big.

○ Honey likes to hop.

4 **What do both rabbits like to eat?**

Possible response: They like to eat hay.

5 **How do the rabbits *not* look the same?**

Possible response: Honey is tan, and Flower is white.

Questions 1–5: Informational Text 2. Identify the main topic and retell key details of a text. Informational Text 3. Describe the connection between two individuals, events, ideas, or pieces of information in a text.

Common Core State Standards

Name _____

Read the selection. Then answer the questions that follow.

Jen Is Six

Jen is six. Mom makes a small cake. Dad has a big red box.   14

What is in it? Mom grins. Dad smiles. Jen has cake. Then Jen   27

looks in the box. It is a hat. Jen likes it!   38

Turn the page.

Answer the questions below.

1 **What happens *first* in the story?**

- ○ Jen gets a hat.
- ● Mom makes a cake.
- ○ Dad has a box.

2 **What happens right *after* Dad smiles?**

- ● Jen has cake.
- ○ Mom grins.
- ○ Dad has a box.

3 **What happens *last* in the story?**

- ○ Dad has a box.
- ○ Mom grins.
- ● Jen looks in the box.

4 **Why do you think the author wrote this story?**

Answers may vary. Possible response: He [She] wants to tell about when Jen is six.

Common Core State Standards

Questions 1–4: Literature 1. Ask and answer questions about key details in a text. **Literature 2.** Retell stories, including key details, and demonstrate understanding of their central message or lesson. **Literature 3.** Describe characters, settings, and major events in a story, using key details.

Fresh Reads Unit 3 Week 1 SI

Name _____

Read the selection. Then answer the questions that follow.

It Is Cold!

Kids like to play in the cold. Big kids skate. They can skate	13
on thick ice. They skate on ponds. Big kids smile.	23
Small kids ride sleds. They can slide down big, slick hills.	34
Sleds go fast! Small kids grin.	40
Then kids go back home. It is time to take a hot bath. Then	54
it is time to take a nap!	61

Turn the page.

- -

Answer the questions below.

1 **What happens *first* in the story?**

○ Small kids ride on sleds.

● Big kids skate on ponds.

○ The kids take a hot bath.

2 **The author wrote this story to**

○ make you feel sad.

○ teach you to skate.

● tell you real things.

3 **What happens in the *middle* of the story?**

● The sleds go fast.

○ The kids go skate.

○ The kids go out to play.

4 **What happens right *after* small kids grin?**

○ The kids take a nap.

○ The kids skate on ice.

● The kids go home.

5 **What happens *last* in the story?**

Possible response: The kids all

take naps.

⌐ **Common Core State Standards** ⌐

Questions 1–5: Literature 1. Ask and answer questions about key details in a text. **Literature 2.** Retell stories, including key details, and demonstrate understanding of their central message or lesson. **Literature 3.** Describe characters, settings, and major events in a story, using key details.

112

Fresh Reads   Unit 3 Week 1 OL

Name _____

Read the selection. Then answer the questions that follow.

Twins Get a Home

Jack has a twin. Jill has a twin. Jack looks like Jill. Jill   13

looks like Jack.   16

Jack and Jill like to sit in the sun. Then Jack and Jill go to   31

a fun home. It has Mom. It has Dad. It has kids. Jack and Jill   46

play with kids. Mom feeds Jack and Jill nice bones.   56

The twins get big fast. Jack is a black dog. What is Jill?   69

Turn the page.

Answer the questions below.

1 **What happens *first* in the story?**

○ The twins go to a fun home.

● The twins sit in the sun.

○ The twins get big fast.

2 **What happens *after* the twins get to the home?**

○ They sit in the sun.

● They play with kids.

○ They are black dogs.

3 **What happens in the *middle* of the story?**

● Mom feeds the twins.

○ Jack looks like Dad.

○ Jill looks like Mom.

4 **What happens *last* in the story?**

The twins get big fast.

5 **Why does the author only tell you the twins are dogs at the *end* of his story?**

Possible response: He wants

to surprise us.

Common Core State Standards

Questions 1–5: Literature 1. Ask and answer questions about key details in a text. **Literature 2.** Retell stories, including key details, and demonstrate understanding of their central message or lesson. **Literature 3.** Describe characters, settings, and major events in a story, using key details.

Fresh Reads   Unit 3 Week 1 A

Read the selection. Then answer the questions that follow.

Dogs and Cats

Kip and Pat are black dogs. Tim and Liz are white cats. | 12

Cats can sit up in trees. Dogs sit under trees. | 22

Tim likes to play with Pat. Liz likes to sit in the sun. | 35

Turn the page.

Answer the questions below.

1 **How are Kip and Pat *alike*?**

○ They can sit in trees.

● They are black dogs.

○ They play with Tim.

2 **How are Tim and Liz *alike*?**

● They are white cats.

○ They do not sit in the sun.

○ They can play with Pat.

3 **How is Tim *not* like Liz?**

○ Tim is a black dog.

● Tim likes to play.

○ Tim sits under trees.

4 **What happens at the *end* of the story?**

Possible response: Liz sits in the sun.

Common Core State Standards

Questions 1–4: Literature 1. Ask and answer questions about key details in a text. **Literature 2.** Retell stories, including key details, and demonstrate understanding of their central message or lesson. **Literature 3.** Describe characters, settings, and major events in a story, using key details. **Literature 9.** Compare and contrast the adventures and experiences of characters in stories.

Name _____

Read the selection. Then answer the questions that follow.

Robin Sings

Robin did not sing. He hummed. He wanted to sing nice | 11

songs like Dove. Robin made a wish. He wished to sing. Then | 23

he sat in a tree and sang! | 30

Cat came to the tree. Cat did not sing. Cat went up in the | 44

tree. Cat sat by Robin. Cat said Robin had a nice song. Robin | 57

was glad to sing at last. | 63

Turn the page.

Answer the questions below.

1 **At the beginning, how is Robin *not* like Dove?**

○ Robin is a bird, and Dove is not.

● Dove can sing, and Robin can not.

○ Robin can sing, and Dove can not.

2 **How are Robin and Cat *alike*?**

○ They can sing a song.

● They sit up in a tree.

○ They make a wish.

3 **How are Cat and Dove *alike*?**

● They are animals.

○ They sing songs.

○ They can hum.

4 **At the end of the story, how are Robin and Dove *alike*?**

○ They sit with the cat.

● They sing nice songs.

○ They wish to hum.

5 **What happens *last* in the story?**

Possible response: Robin is glad that he can sing.

Common Core State Standards

Questions 1–4: Literature 1. Ask and answer questions about key details in a text. **Literature 2.** Retell stories, including key details, and demonstrate understanding of their central message or lesson. **Literature 3.** Describe characters, settings, and major events in a story, using key details. **Literature 9.** Compare and contrast the adventures and experiences of characters in stories.

Fresh Reads   Unit 3 Week 2 OL

Name _____

Read the selection. Then answer the questions that follow.

A Nice Spot

Lin and Rose will make a nice spot to sit. Lin rakes up | 13
leaves. Work makes Lin hot. He stops to rest. Rose digs up | 25
weeds. | 26

Lin takes the leaves. He drops them in a big bag. Rose sets | 39
the weeds in a big can. | 45

Lin and Rose sit in the nice spot they made. Lin smiles at | 58
Rose. Rose grins at Lin. | 63

Turn the page.

Answer the questions below.

1 What happens at the _beginning_ of the story?

● Lin rakes the leaves.

○ Lin smiles at Rose.

○ Lin drops leaves in a bag.

2 How is Lin _not_ like Rose?

○ He sits in a nice spot.

● He rakes up leaves.

○ He digs up the weeds.

3 How are Lin and Rose _alike_?

○ They rake the leaves.

○ They dig the weeds.

● They sit in one spot.

4 How is Rose _not_ like Lin?

Possible response: Rose digs weeds.

5 What do Lin and Rose like to do?

Answers may vary. Possible response:

They like to sit in a nice spot.

Common Core State Standards

Question 1: Literature 1. Ask and answer questions about key details in a text. **Questions 2–5: Literature 3.** Describe characters, settings, and major events in a story, using key details. **Literature 9.** Compare and contrast the adventures and experiences of characters in stories.

Name _____

Read the selection. Then answer the questions that follow.

Red Foxes

Red foxes are small like cats. Red foxes have nice fur. They   12

can live in many places. Red foxes eat fish and mice. But red   25

foxes are not good pets.   30

Turn the page.

Answer the questions below.

1 Which is a statement of opinion?

● Red foxes have nice fur.

○ Red foxes are small like cats.

○ Red foxes can eat mice.

2 Which is a statement of fact?

● Red foxes eat fish and mice.

○ Red foxes are not good pets.

○ Red foxes have nice fur.

3 Which is a statement of opinion?

○ Red foxes live in many places.

● Red foxes are not good pets.

○ Red foxes can eat fish.

4 How are red foxes and cats *alike*?

Possible response: They are small.

Common Core State Standards

Questions 1–3: Informational Text 1. Ask and answer questions about key details in a text. **Question 4: Informational Text 3.** Describe the connection between two individuals, events, ideas, or pieces of information in a text.

Name _____

Read the selection. Then answer the questions that follow.

Hogs

Hogs are pigs. Hogs and pigs are called swine. Hogs live	11
in big pens called lots. Hogs will sit in the mud when they get	25
hot.	26
Hogs have thick skin and no fur. Hog skin can be black.	38
Hog skin can be white. It can be red too. Hogs can also have	52
spots.	53
Hogs look very nice. They smell good. They dig for bugs.	64
Hogs are fun to watch!	69

Turn the page.

Answer the questions below.

1 **Which is a statement of fact from the selection?**

● Hogs live in big pens called lots.

○ Hogs are fun to watch!

○ Hogs look very nice.

2 **It is a statement of opinion that**

○ hogs have no fur.

○ hogs sit in the mud.

● hogs smell good.

3 **Which is a statement of opinion?**

○ Hog skin can have spots.

● It is fun to watch hogs.

○ Hogs dig for bugs.

4 **Which is a statement of fact in the selection?**

● Hog skin can be white.

○ Hogs look very nice.

○ They smell good.

5 **What is the *same* about hogs and pigs?**

Possible response: Hogs and pigs are called swine.

1 Copyright © Pearson Education, Inc., or its affiliates. All Rights Reserved.

Common Core State Standards

Questions 1–4: Informational Text 1. Ask and answer questions about key details in a text. **Question 5: Informational Text 3.** Describe the connection between two individuals, events, ideas, or pieces of information in a text.

Name _____

Read the selection. Then answer the questions that follow.

Make a Car

Your family can make fun cars to play with at home. Get a | 13

box you can cut up and color. You can also use a plastic milk | 27

jug. Make fake wheels from plastic. Make stripes on the sides | 38

to make the car look like it can go fast. | 48

You made a nice hot rod! You can race cars with your best | 61

friends and family. | 64

Turn the page.

Answer the questions below.

1 **Which is a statement of fact?**

- ○ You can make fun cars.
- ● A car can be made from a box.
- ○ Hot rods are nice to make.

2 **It is a statement of opinion that**

- ○ you can make fake wheels.
- ○ you can use plastic to make cars.
- ● box cars make good hot rods.

3 **What is a statement of opinion?**

- ● You made a nice hot rod!
- ○ You can race cars with friends.
- ○ You can also use a milk jug.

4 **Write a statement of fact based on the selection.**

Answers may vary. Possible response:

You can use a box to make a car.

5 **How are boxes and milk jugs *alike*?**

Possible response: You can use them to

make race cars.

Common Core State Standards

Questions 1–4: Informational Text 1. Ask and answer questions about key details in a text. **Question 5: Informational Text 3.** Describe the connection between two individuals, events, ideas, or pieces of information in a text.

Name _____

Read the selection. Then answer the questions that follow.

Ann Bakes a Cake

Ann said, "Mom, I want to bake a cake." | 9

Mom said, "I will help you make it." | 17

Ann got a box. It had cake mix in it. Mom got eggs. Mom | 31

and Ann made a nice big cake. | 38

Turn the page.

Answer the questions below.

1 **Why do you think the author wrote "Ann Bakes a Cake"?**

○ to tell about a cake

○ to tell about eggs

● to tell a good story

2 **How did the author show you Ann likes to bake?**

○ She ate an egg.

● She made a cake.

○ She got a box.

3 **This story was**

● just for some fun.

○ to make you feel sad.

○ all about how to bake.

4 **What did Mom do _after_ Ann got a box?**

Possible response: Mom got eggs.

⌐ **Common Core State Standards** ⌐

Questions 1–4: Literature 1. Ask and answer questions about key details in a text. **Literature 2.** Retell stories, including key details, and demonstrate understanding of their central message or lesson. **Literature 3.** Describe characters, settings, and major events in a story, using key details.

Fresh Reads   Unit 3 Week 4 SI

Name _____

Read the selection. Then answer the questions that follow.

Fun in the Sun

One fine day, Rob and Tom woke up. It was sunny and	12
nice. Rob said, "Get up quick, Tom." Tom got up fast. They	24
felt happy! They had all day to spend with Dad.	34
Dad said, "We can ride bikes on the trail by the lake."	46
Rob grinned. Tom smiled. The small bikes fit in the back of	58
the truck. Then Dad drove Rob and Tom to the big lake. They	71
all had lots of fun in the hot sun.	80

Turn the page.

Answer the questions below.

1 **Why did the author write this story?**

○ to tell about bikes

○ to tell about a lake

● to tell about a fun time

2 **What happens in this story?**

● A family rides bikes.

○ Dad gets an old bike.

○ It rains on them all day.

3 **How do you think the author feels about bikes?**

○ He is scared of them.

● He likes to ride them.

○ He wishes he had one.

4 **How does the author let you know that Rob and Tom wanted to ride bikes?**

○ Rob frowned and Tom cried.

● Rob grinned and Tom smiled.

○ Dad drove to the big lake.

5 **How can you tell Rob and Tom were in the same family?**

Possible response: They spend the day with Dad.

Common Core State Standards

Questions 1–5: **Literature 1.** Ask and answer questions about key details in a text. **Literature 2.** Retell stories, including key details, and demonstrate understanding of their central message or lesson. **Literature 3.** Describe characters, settings, and major events in a story, using key details.

Name _____

Read the selection. Then answer the questions that follow.

Brave Frog

Frog did not like rain at all. When it rained, Frog did not	13
feel safe. He ran to hide. Then it rained hard and did not stop.	27
Frog hid fast.	30
Then Frog saw Squirrel in a box. Squirrel needed help to	41
get safe. Rain filled the box up to his neck! Frog had to help	55
fast.	56
Frog ran in the rain. Frog got Squirrel out of the box. Frog	69
saved Squirrel. Then Frog felt safe in the rain.	78

Turn the page.

Answer the questions below.

1 **What was this story about?**

- ○ a squirrel that liked rain
- ● a frog that saved a squirrel
- ○ a girl that needed help

2 **What did the author think about Frog?**

- ○ Frog was silly.
- ○ Frog was sad.
- ● Frog was brave.

3 **How does the author let you know that Frog has changed?**

- ● She says that Frog felt safe.
- ○ She says that Frog saw Squirrel.
- ○ She says that Frog hid fast.

4 **Why do you think the author wrote this story?**

Possible response: She wants you to learn to be brave like Frog.

5 **What was a lesson for Frog?**

Possible response: Frog could feel safe in the rain.

Common Core State Standards

Questions 1–5: **Literature 1.** Ask and answer questions about key details in a text. **Literature 2.** Retell stories, including key details, and demonstrate understanding of their central message or lesson. **Literature 3.** Describe characters, settings, and major events in a story, using key details.

Name _____

Read the selection. Then answer the questions that follow.

Take a Ride

Cars and trucks run fast. It is fun to ride in cars. Trains run   14

on tracks. They are quick. Planes fly fast in the sky. It is the   28

most fun to take a ride in a plane!   37

Turn the page.

Answer the questions below.

1 **Which is a statement of fact?**

○ Cars are fun to ride in.

○ Planes are the most fun.

● Trains run on tracks.

2 **Which is a statement of opinion?**

○ Trucks run fast like cars.

● It is fun to go for car rides.

○ Planes fly fast in the sky.

3 **What does the selection tell about *last*?**

○ cars

● planes

○ trains

4 **What is a statement of opinion about planes in the selection?**

Possible response: Planes are the most fun to ride in.

Common Core State Standards

Questions 1–4: Informational Text 1. Ask and answer questions about key details in a text.

Name _____

Read the selection. Then answer the questions that follow.

Ants

Ants make nice homes. They dig deep in the ground to | 11

make homes. Ants can make hills for homes too. Ant hills stick | 23

up on top of the ground. | 29

Ants live in a big family. They work all the time. Ants walk | 42

far to get food. They take it back home to feed others. | 54

Big ants keep ant eggs safe. Baby ants hatch from the eggs. | 66

Baby ants are cute. | 70

Ants are fun to watch! | 75

Turn the page.

Answer the questions below.

1 **What is a statement of opinion?**

- ○ Ants live in a family.
- ● Baby ants are cute.
- ○ Ants keep eggs safe.

2 **What happens *first*?**

- ● Ants make homes.
- ○ Ants walk for food.
- ○ Ants keep eggs safe.

3 **What is a statement of fact?**

- ○ Ants are fun to watch.
- ● Ants take food home.
- ○ Ants make nice homes.

4 **What sentence tells a statement of opinion?**

- ○ Big ants keep ant eggs safe.
- ○ Ant hills stick up on top of the ground.
- ● Ants are fun to watch.

5 **What is a statement of fact about baby ants?**

Possible response: Baby ants hatch from eggs.

Common Core State Standards

Questions 1–5: Informational Text 1. Ask and answer questions about key details in a text.

Name _____

Read the selection. Then answer the questions that follow.

Green Trees

Some trees get green leaves first. In the fall, the leaves turn	12
red or yellow. They are pretty. Then they drop on the ground.	24
Kids use leaves to make art.	30
Some trees are green all the time. They are called evergreen	41
trees. Some of them are small. Others grow very big.	51
Animals like evergreen trees. Birds like to sit in them.	61
Rabbits make homes under them. People like evergreen trees	70
too. Evergreen trees look nice and smell good.	78

Turn the page.

Answer the questions below.

1 **What happens *last* to some tree leaves?**

- ● They fall on the ground.
- ○ They turn red or yellow.
- ○ They grow out green.

2 **What tells a statement of opinion?**

- ○ Rabbits can live under trees.
- ○ Trees have green leaves first.
- ● Some trees smell very good.

3 **What tells a statement of fact?**

- ○ The red leaves are pretty.
- ● Some trees are green all the time.
- ○ Evergreen trees look nice.

4 **What is a statement of opinion about leaves?**

Possible response: The colors of the leaves are pretty.

5 **Write a statement of fact about evergreen trees.**

Possible response: Some of them get tall.

Common Core State Standards

Questions 1–5: Informational Text 1. Ask and answer questions about key details in a text.

Name _____

Read the selection. Then answer the questions that follow.

Twins

Jane and Mark are twins. Jane was born first. Mark is   11

bigger than Jane. Jane likes to play ball and swim. Mark likes   23

to brush his dog when it is dirty. Mark likes to pet his cat. Jane   38

and Mark like to make forts.   44

Turn the page.

Answer the questions below.

1 How are Mark and Jane the *same*?

○ They are girls.

● They make forts.

○ They swim fast.

2 What do you know about Jane and Mark?

○ They are not very tall.

○ They like to run races.

● They are in one family.

3 What can you tell about Mark?

● He likes animals.

○ He has a horse.

○ He can't swim.

4 How do you know Jane likes to be outside?

Possible response: She likes to play ball and swim.

Common Core State Standards

Question 1: Literature 9. Compare and contrast the adventures and experiences of characters in stories. **Questions 2–4: Literature 1.** Ask and answer questions about key details in a text. **Literature 3.** Describe characters, settings, and major events in a story, using key details.

Name _____

Read the selection. Then answer the questions that follow.

A New Place

Jake had to go live in a new place. Mom got a new job.	14
Jake felt sad and just sat on his bed. Then he sat on the rug.	29
Dad came to see him. Dad sat by Jake and hugged him.	41
Then Jake felt much better. He felt glad for Mom.	51
Jake went to a new school. He met Tim and Jack in the first	65
week. They all liked to play ball. Jake felt happy at last.	77

Turn the page.

Answer the questions below.

1 **Dad wanted to**

● help Jake.

○ play with Jake.

○ trick Jake.

2 **What made Jake feel sad?**

● He did not want to go to a new place.

○ He had to stay home from school.

○ He would miss his Mom and Dad.

3 **How was Mom the *same* as Dad?**

○ She got a new job.

● She was glad to go.

○ She hugged Jake.

4 **Why was Jake happy at last?**

Possible response: He met Tim and Jack.

5 **How do you think Jake met Tim and Jack?**

Possible response: Jake made new friends at his new school.

Common Core State Standards

Questions 1, 2, 4, 5: Literature 1. Ask and answer questions about key details in a text. **Literature 3.** Describe characters, settings, and major events in a story, using key details. **Question 3: Literature 9.** Compare and contrast the adventures and experiences of characters in stories.

Read the selection. Then answer the questions that follow.

Games

Ben liked to play all games. He liked hide-and-seek best.	10
His sister Kris liked to hide. She liked Ben to look for her.	23
Dad liked to take Ben to ball games. Ben had lots of fun	36
with Dad at the games.	41
Mom liked to sing with Ben and Kris. Mom made up a	53
singing game. Mom sang one part. Then Ben and Kris would	64
take turns adding the rest. They all liked this fun game!	75

Turn the page.

Answer the questions below.

1 **Why does Ben like all games?**

● He likes to have fun.

○ He likes to play with Kris.

○ He likes to be outside.

2 **What makes Kris happy?**

○ to look for Ben

○ to go to ball games

● to hide from Ben

3 **How are Dad and Mom the *same*?**

○ They like to go to ball games.

● They like to play with the kids.

○ They like to sing together.

4 **Why do you think Ben likes hide-and-seek best?**

Possible response: He likes it because Kris makes it fun to play.

5 **Why do you think Ben likes ball games?**

Possible response: Ben likes to spend time with his dad.

Common Core State Standards

Questions 1, 2, 4, 5: Literature 1. Ask and answer questions about key details in a text. Literature 3. Describe characters, settings, and major events in a story, using key details. Question 3: Literature 9. Compare and contrast the adventures and experiences of characters in stories.

Name _____

Read the selection. Then answer the questions that follow.

Plants

Many people like seeing green plants inside. All plants | 9

need lots of sun and nice fresh water. Outside plants get plenty | 21

of sunshine and rain. When plants stay inside, people must | 31

water them and place them in the sun at times. | 41

Turn the page.

Answer the questions below.

1 Sunshine makes plants

○ dark.

○ cold.

● grow.

2 What can happen if plants do not get water?

● The plants will not live.

○ The plants will become green.

○ The plants will get flowers.

3 Why do many people have plants in the house?

○ They want to have food around.

● They enjoy growing plants inside.

○ They need to have some water.

4 Why do people have to water inside plants?

Answers may vary. Possible response: Plants that grow inside do not get rain like outside plants do.

Common Core State Standards

Questions 1–4: Informational Text 1. Ask and answer questions about key details in a text. **Informational Text 3.** Describe the connection between two individuals, events, ideas, or pieces of information in a text.

Name _____

Read the selection. Then answer the questions that follow.

Selling Flowers

Bob came to the park every week to sell picked flowers. He	12
called, "Fresh flowers for sale!"	17
Lee said, "Sell me ten red roses."	24
"No red roses for sale," said Bob. "I can sell you red mums	37
or a nice daisy."	41
"I just like roses," said Lee. "I do not want mums or a	54
daisy."	55
Bob came back the next week. He had ten red roses to sell	68
to Lee.	70
Lee said, "I do not want roses. I will take ten red mums and	84
one nice, fresh daisy."	88

Turn the page.

Answer the questions below.

1 **Why did Bob come to the park?**

● to sell flowers

○ to visit his family

○ to meet his friends

2 **Why didn't Lee take a daisy?**

○ She likes flowers.

● She wanted roses.

○ She wanted mums.

3 **Why did Bob bring roses the next week?**

● Lee asked for them.

○ He liked red flowers best.

○ Lee wanted a daisy.

4 **Why didn't Lee get roses the next week?**

○ She did not like roses.

○ She had gotten roses before.

● She wanted mums now.

5 **How do you think Bob felt when Lee did not take the roses?**

Possible response: He was not happy.

Common Core State Standards

Questions 1–5: **Literature 1.** Ask and answer questions about key details in a text. **Literature 2.** Retell stories, including key details, and demonstrate understanding of their central message or lesson. **Literature 3.** Describe characters, settings, and major events in a story, using key details.

Name _____

Read the selection. Then answer the questions that follow.

The Party

Beth was new on our block. She liked us, so she had a	13
party for us at her home. It was lots of fun!	24
Beth had made a piñata for us to hit. It was shaped like a	38
big red dog. We all got turns hitting it. It did not crack. Then	52
Beth hit it harder. It broke in two! Small bags fell on the	65
ground. We all got little bags. There were fun things to play	77
with inside the bags.	81
Then Beth let us make a piñata!	88

Turn the page.

- -

Fresh Reads Unit 4 Week 1 A

Answer the questions below.

1 **Why did Beth have a party?**

- ○ It was her mother's birthday.
- ○ The family told her to do it.
- ● She wanted to make friends.

2 **Why did they hit the piñata?**

- ● to break it open
- ○ to make it bark
- ○ to spin it around

3 **What happened when Beth hit the piñata harder?**

- ○ It came down.
- ○ It did not crack.
- ● Bags fell out.

4 **Why did they all go to Beth's party?**

Possible response: They wanted to have a fun time.

5 **How did Beth feel after the party ended?**

Possible response: She was happy they all had fun.

Name _____

Read the selection. Then answer the questions that follow.

Two Birds

Robin did not like to share his tree. His friend	10
Hummingbird needed a place to make a nest. She said,	20
"Robin, you can stay in your nest by the trunk. I will make my	34
nest in the branches. That way, we can stay in the same tree	47
and be happy."	50

Turn the page.

Answer the questions below.

1 **What is this story trying to teach?**

- ○ a way to make a nest
- ● a way to share with others
- ○ a way to be like a bird

2 **What is the big idea in this story?**

- ● sharing
- ○ robins
- ○ eating

3 **What would be another good name for this story?**

- ○ Bugs in the Trees
- ○ Having Friends
- ● Working Together

4 **How were the two birds able to live in the same tree together?**

Answers may vary. Possible response: Each bird stayed in its own place in the tree.

1 Copyright © Pearson Education, Inc., or its affiliates. All Rights Reserved.

Common Core State Standards

Questions 1–3: Literature 2. Retell stories, including key details, and demonstrate understanding of their central message or lesson.
Question 4: Literature 3. Describe characters, settings, and major events in a story, using key details. **Literature 9.** Compare and contrast the adventures and experiences of characters in stories.

Read the selection. Then answer the questions that follow.

Sun and Sea

Sea felt sad. She needed friends. All she could see was the	12
sun and land.	15
Then Sun called to Sea. "Hi! Can you play with me?"	26
"But you are up in the sky," said Sea. "How can we play?"	39
Sun said, "I can shine on land and on sea. I can smile at	53
you."	54
Sea said, "I can splash and wave at you! We can be	66
friends."	67
Sea splashed and waved at Sun every day. Sun shone on	78
Sea and smiled when she splashed. They had fun.	87

Turn the page.

Answer the questions below.

1 When did Sun and Sea play together?

- ○ in the dark
- ● in the day
- ○ at night

2 What is this story all about?

- ● working together to make friends
- ○ saying good-bye
- ○ splashing and talking

3 Sea and Sun had to find a way to

- ○ be sad.
- ● play together.
- ○ go up and down.

4 What does this story teach you about friends?

- ● Friends can help each other.
- ○ Friends need to stay far away.
- ○ Friends can be mean.

5 How did Sun and Sea become friends?

Possible response: They came up with a plan for how to play together.

Common Core State Standards

Question 1: Literature 1. Ask and answer questions about key details in a text. Questions 2–4: Literature 2. Retell stories, including key details, and demonstrate understanding of their central message or lesson. Literature 9. Compare and contrast the adventures and experiences of characters in stories. Question 5: Literature 3. Describe characters, settings, and major events in a story, using key details.

Name _____

Read the selection. Then answer the questions that follow.

Greg's First Art Show

Greg hopes to be a fine artist. To help him do that, he plans | 14

to show his art to people. | 20

Greg thinks he will try new ways to make art. He splashes | 32

paint on bags and uses many colors and shapes. He makes | 43

shapes such as green boxes and red lines. He adds white | 54

stripes and black dots. | 58

At last Greg makes signs for his show. Lots of people come | 70

to see his art. They like it very much and tell Greg he will be a | 86

great artist one day. | 90

Turn the page.

Answer the questions below.

1 **What is the big idea in this story?**

○ working with others

● growing as an artist

○ getting paintings on sale

2 **What does Greg learn from painting?**

○ to make people happy

● to try new things

○ to sell big signs

3 **What would be another good name for this story?**

● A New Artist

○ Greg's School

○ How to Make Paints

4 **What does this story teach you?**

Possible response: When you try new things, you learn more.

5 **Why does Greg make signs for his show?**

He wants to have people come to see his art.

Common Core State Standards

Question 1: **Literature 1.** Ask and answer questions about key details in a text. Questions 2–4: **Literature 2.** Retell stories, including key details, and demonstrate understanding of their central message or lesson. **Literature 9.** Compare and contrast the adventures and experiences of characters in stories. Question 5: **Literature 3.** Describe characters, settings, and major events in a story, using key details.

Name _____

Read the selection. Then answer the questions that follow.

Into the Sky!

At one time, people stayed on land or sea. We rode in cars | 13

or trains or ships. Then we made planes. Planes let us fly a | 26

long way in a short time. Planes can be very big. Lots of us | 40

can fit in them. Flying is fun! | 47

Turn the page.

Answer the questions below.

1 **What helps people move into the sky?**

○ ships

○ cars

● planes

2 **Why is flying a good way to get places?**

○ It is bigger.

● It is faster.

○ It is longer.

3 **What do big planes do?**

● fly many people

○ stay on the land

○ float on the sea

4 **What is a statement of opinion about flying?**

Possible response: Flying is

fun!

Common Core State Standards

Questions 1–4: Informational Text 1. Ask and answer questions about key details in a text. **Informational Text 2.** Identify the main topic and retell key details of a text.

Name _____

Read the selection. Then answer the questions that follow.

Pick a Pet

It can be hard to pick a pet. Many animals make good pets.	13
You may wish for a pet with soft fur. Cats and dogs can	26
play with you inside or outside. Gerbils stay in cages much of	38
the time, like birds. You may wish for birds or fish. Birds have	51
colored feathers. Fish need to be in water.	59
Every pet needs good food and a safe home. It can be hard	72
to pick the best pet for you!	79

Turn the page.

Answer the questions below.

1 **What sentence tells a statement of opinion?**

- ○ Gerbils stay in cages much of the time.
- ● It can be hard to pick a pet.
- ○ Birds have colored feathers.

2 **Why do cats and dogs make good pets?**

- ○ They need food to eat.
- ● They play with people.
- ○ They need a safe home.

3 **What animal needs to live in water?**

- ○ cat
- ○ dog
- ● fish

4 **What is a pet that stays in a cage?**

- ○ a fish
- ● a bird
- ○ a cat

5 **What does every pet need?**

Possible response: Pets need good food and a safe home.

Common Core State Standards

Questions 1–5: **Informational Text 1.** Ask and answer questions about key details in a text. **Informational Text 2.** Identify the main topic and retell key details of a text.

Name _____

Read the selection. Then answer the questions that follow.

Shells

Shells are hard cases that were part of a sea animal at one	13
time. It is lots of fun to go to sunny, sandy beaches and hunt	27
for shells. You can also get shells in muddy places. After a	39
storm is the best time to hunt for shells. Make sure the place	52
you go lets people pick up shells and take them home. You	64
might pick up clam shells or snail shells. Some people hunt	75
shells for a hobby. All shells look better and feel better when	87
you clean them well.	91

Turn the page.

Answer the questions below.

1 **What are shells?**

○ muddy places

● parts of animals

○ sandy beaches

2 **Where can you hunt for shells?**

● on a beach

○ at your home

○ in hard cases

3 **What shells could you find?**

○ whale shells

○ fish shells

● clam shells

4 **What should you do before you take shells home?**

Possible response: Make sure it
is all right to take them with you.

5 **What is a statement of opinion about shells?**

Possible response: Shells look
better when they are clean.

Common Core State Standards

Questions 1–5: Informational Text 1. Ask and answer questions about key details in a text. **Informational Text 2.** Identify the main topic and retell key details of a text.

Name _____

Read the selection. Then answer the questions that follow.

Dog and Cat

Dog did not like Cat near him. But Cat did not leave Dog.	13
Cat said, "I just like being near dogs."	21
Dog ran after Cat. Cat went up a tree fast. Cat said, "Why	34
did you chase me?"	38
Dog said, "I just like to chase cats!"	46

Turn the page.

Answer the questions below.

1 **Where did Cat run?**

- ○ into the park
- ● up a tree
- ○ down a street

2 **What did Dog want Cat to do?**

- ● leave him
- ○ run with him
- ○ chase him

3 **Why did Dog chase Cat?**

- ○ because Cat liked it
- ○ so that Cat would talk
- ● because Dog liked it

4 **How were Dog and Cat the *same*?**

Possible response: They were both stubborn.

Common Core State Standards

Questions 1–3: Literature 1. Ask and answer questions about key details in a text. **Literature 3.** Describe characters, settings, and major events in a story, using key details. **Question 4: Literature 9.** Compare and contrast the adventures and experiences of characters in stories.

Name _____

Read the selection. Then answer the questions that follow.

Big Fish in a Small Lake

A little fish had a nice home in a small lake. He got bigger	14
very fast, until he was the biggest fish in the lake. Still he kept	28
growing bigger. He named himself Big Fish. He needed a	38
bigger home.	40
Big Fish swam and splashed to the far end of the lake. He	53
swam fast and then jumped up high. He sailed far! When Big	65
Fish landed, he was in the deep blue sea. He swam in the sea	79
and saw many fish bigger than he. Big Fish seemed small in	91
the big sea.	94

Turn the page.

Answer the questions below.

1 **Where did the fish live at the *beginning* of the story?**

○ in the big sea

● in a small lake

○ in a deep pond

2 **Why did the fish want to leave?**

○ He wanted to see more places.

○ He liked to fly up in the air.

● He needed a bigger home.

3 **How did the fish get to his new place?**

○ He swam over to it.

● He jumped far.

○ He walked there.

4 **Where did the fish live at the *end* of the story?**

○ in the air

○ on the land

● in the sea

5 **How did the fish feel *after* he moved?**

Possible response: He felt like a little fish, not a big fish.

Common Core State Standards

Questions 1–5: **Literature 1.** Ask and answer questions about key details in a text. **Literature 3.** Describe characters, settings, and major events in a story, using key details.

166

Name _____

Read the selection. Then answer the questions that follow.

Fun Club

Dear Dad,	2
Will you take me to the Fun Club? It starts in three days,	15
and we will have lots of fun. We can see many things. We can	29
hear the caterpillar sing. We can see the pig paint its art and	42
then see it fly in the sky. We can feel the goat with red spots.	57
Then we can eat green grapes. They will be yummy! I know	69
we will find things we have never seen. Can we go, Dad? Let	82
me know what you think. Mom will help us plan the trip.	94
Love,	95
Jeff	96

Turn the page.

Answer the questions below.

1 Jeff wants to go to the club with

- ● Dad.
- ○ Mom.
- ○ friends.

2 What animal paints?

- ○ a goat
- ● a pig
- ○ a caterpillar

3 What will Jeff eat at the club?

- ○ candy
- ● grapes
- ○ corn

4 How does Jeff tell about the Fun Club?

Possible response: He writes
a letter.

5 How are the pig and the caterpillar *alike*?

Possible response: They both
do things that people do.

Common Core State Standards

Questions 1–4: Literature 1. Ask and answer questions about key details in a text. Literature 3. Describe characters, settings, and major events in a story, using key details. Question 5: Literature 9. Compare and contrast the adventures and experiences of characters in stories.

Name _____

Read the selection. Then answer the questions that follow.

Sunny Day

Max played in the sunshine. He liked to play by himself.	11
Then Carl came over. "May I play with you?" he asked.	22
Max said, "Yes!"	25
Carl and Max had fun. Max liked playing with Carl. It was	37
more fun to play with friends than to play by himself.	48

Turn the page.

Answer the questions below.

1 **What is the big idea in this story?**

○ Summer days are long and hot.

● Playing with others is better.

○ Being outside is good for boys.

2 **What does this story show readers?**

○ how to play by yourself

○ some games for two friends

● a way to have more fun

3 **What would be another good name for this story?**

● Fun with a Friend

○ Happy School Days

○ The Summer Games

4 **From this story, what can you tell that Carl likes to do?**

Possible response: Carl likes to play with Max.

Common Core State Standards

Questions 1–3: Literature 2. Retell stories, including key details, and demonstrate understanding of their central message or lesson.
Question 4: Literature 1. Ask and answer questions about key details in a text. **Literature 3.** Describe characters, settings, and major events in a story, using key details.

Name _____

Read the selection. Then answer the questions that follow.

At the Park

Fred went to the park with his mom. He got on the swing	13
and stayed there. "Fred, share the swing," called his mom.	23
Fred did not share.	27
Jimmy played ball at the park. His mom called, "Jimmy,	37
share the ball." Jimmy did not share.	44
"May, share the jump rope," called her mom. May did not	55
share.	56
Then Kathy came to the park. She said, "We can all make a	69
neat fort if we work together. Come and have fun with me."	81
The kids came to help. They all made a fort and had fun	94
playing together.	96

Turn the page.

Answer the questions below.

1 **What is the big idea in this story?**

◯ It is good to jump rope.

◯ It is hard to make a fort.

● It is fun to play together.

2 **What is this story trying to teach?**

◯ how to make a neat set of swings

● how to share and play with others

◯ how to use snow to put up a fort

3 **What do the kids learn from Kathy?**

● Sharing is more fun than playing alone.

◯ They need more than one jump rope.

◯ Fred should take turns on the swing.

4 **What would be a good name for this story?**

◯ How to Play Ball

◯ Jump Rope Tricks

● Playing Together

5 **Why do the mothers tell their kids to share things?**

Possible response: They want them to be nice to others.

Common Core State Standards

Questions 1–4: Literature 1. Ask and answer questions about key details in a text. **Literature 2.** Retell stories, including key details, and demonstrate understanding of their central message or lesson. **Question 5: Literature 3.** Describe characters, settings, and major events in a story, using key details.

Name _____

Cinderella

Read the selection. Then answer the questions that follow.

Greg's First Art Show

Greg hopes to be a fine artist. To help him do that, he plans to show his art to people.

Greg thinks he will try new ways to make art. He splashes paint on bags and uses many colors and shapes. He makes shapes such as green boxes and red lines. He adds white stripes and black dots.

At last Greg makes signs for his show. Lots of people come to see his art. They like it very much and tell Greg he will be a great artist one day.

14
20
32
43
54
58
70
86
90

Turn the page.

Fresh Reads Unit 4 Week 2 A

155

Read the selection. Then answer the questions that follow.

Greg's First Art Show

Greg hopes to be a fine artist. To help him do that, he plans to show his art to people.

Greg thinks he will try new ways to make art. He splashes paint on bags and uses many colors and shapes. He makes shapes such as green boxes and red lines. He adds white stripes and black dots.

At last Greg makes signs for his show. Lots of people come to see his art. They like it very much and tell Greg he will be a great artist one day.

Turn the page.

Answer the questions below.

1 **What is the big idea in this story?**

○ working with others

○ growing as an artist

○ getting paintings on sale

2 **What does Greg learn from painting?**

○ to make people happy

○ to try new things

○ to sell big signs

3 **What would be another good name for this story?**

○ A New Artist

○ Greg's School

○ How to Make Paints

4 **What does this story teach you?**

_____

- -

_____

- -

_____

5 **Why does Greg make signs for his show?**

_____

- -

_____

- -

_____

- -

Name _____

Read the selection. Then answer the questions that follow.

Sun and Sea

Sea felt sad. She needed friends. All she could see was the	12
sun and land.	15
Then Sun called to Sea. "Hi! Can you play with me?"	26
"But you are up in the sky," said Sea. "How can we play?"	39
Sun said, "I can shine on land and on sea. I can smile at	53
you."	54
Sea said, "I can splash and wave at you! We can be	66
friends."	67
Sea splashed and waved at Sun every day. Sun shone on	78
Sea and smiled when she splashed. They had fun.	87

Turn the page.

Name _____

Read the selection. Then answer the questions that follow.

Sun and Sea

Sea felt sad. She needed friends. All she could see was the sun and land.

Then Sun called to Sea. "Hi! Can you play with me?"

"But you are up in the sky," said Sea. "How can we play?"

Sun said, "I can shine on land and on sea. I can smile at you."

Sea said, "I can splash and wave at you! We can be friends."

Sea splashed and waved at Sun every day. Sun shone on Sea and smiled when she splashed. They had fun.

Turn the page.

Answer the questions below.

1 **When did Sun and Sea play together?**

○ in the dark

○ in the day

○ at night

2 **What is this story all about?**

○ working together to make friends

○ saying good-bye

○ splashing and talking

3 **Sea and Sun had to find a way to**

○ be sad.

○ play together.

○ go up and down.

4 **What does this story teach you about friends?**

○ Friends can help each other.

○ Friends need to stay far away.

○ Friends can be mean.

5 **How did Sun and Sea become friends?**

_____

- -

_____

- -

_____

- -

154

Name _____

Read the selection. Then answer the questions that follow.

Two Birds

Robin did not like to share his tree. His friend	10
Hummingbird needed a place to make a nest. She said,	20
"Robin, you can stay in your nest by the trunk. I will make my	34
nest in the branches. That way, we can stay in the same tree	47
and be happy."	50

Turn the page.

Name _____

Read the selection. Then answer the questions that follow.

Two Birds

Robin did not like to share his tree. His friend Hummingbird needed a place to make a nest. She said, "Robin, you can stay in your nest by the trunk. I will make my nest in the branches. That way, we can stay in the same tree and be happy."

Turn the page.

Answer the questions below.

1 **What is this story trying to teach?**

    ◯ a way to make a nest

    ◯ a way to share with others

    ◯ a way to be like a bird

2 **What is the big idea in this story?**

    ◯ sharing

    ◯ robins

    ◯ eating

3 **What would be another good name for this story?**

    ◯ Bugs in the Trees

    ◯ Having Friends

    ◯ Working Together

4 **How were the two birds able to live in the same tree together?**

_____

_____

_____

_____

_____

_____

_____

Name _____

Read the selection. Then answer the questions that follow.

Jane's Visit

Mom drove Jane to the animal shelter every week. When	10
Jane got there, she went to see the cats first. She petted all the	24
cats and gave them fresh water. Jane teased the cats with a	36
long string. She smiled at them when they ran to catch it.	48
Then Jane and Mom went outside to play ball with the	59
dogs. Jane made sure each dog got a pat on the head and a	73
treat from the big jar. Then she took them out for a quick trot	87
on a leash one at a time. When Jane left, she told the pets she	102
would come back soon.	106

Turn the page.

Answer the questions below.

1 **What is the big idea in this story?**

- ○ playing with your cat
- ○ feeding the pet animals
- ● helping out at a shelter

2 **What does this story show the reader?**

- ○ You must talk to animals.
- ● It can be fun to be a helper.
- ○ The dogs are the most fun.

3 **What is another good name for this story?**

- ○ Pick the Right Pet
- ● Helping Cats and Dogs
- ○ How to Walk a Dog

4 **What has Jane learned from going to the shelter?**

Possible response: It feels good to help animals.

5 **How do you know that Jane likes going to the shelter?**

Possible response: She visits there every week.

Common Core State Standards

Questions 1–4: Literature 1. Ask and answer questions about key details in a text. **Literature 2.** Retell stories, including key details, and demonstrate understanding of their central message or lesson. **Question 5: Literature 3.** Describe characters, settings, and major events in a story, using key details.

Name _____

Read the selection. Then answer the questions that follow.

Dance Class

Ling did not like dance class. Kids made fun of her.	11
Every week she asked, "Dad, must I go?"	19
Dad felt sad. He wished Ling liked class.	27
Dad said, "Just do your best, and the kids will be nice."	39
He was right! Ling felt happy.	45

Turn the page.

Answer the questions below.

1 How did Ling feel at the *beginning* of the story?

○ happy
○ afraid
● sad

2 Why didn't Ling like her dance class?

● Other kids picked on her.
○ The class was too hard.
○ Dad made her go to class.

3 What made Ling's father sad?

○ He did not want Ling to dance.
○ He did not like to drive Ling to class.
● Ling did not like the dance class.

4 What made Ling happy at the *end* of the story?

Possible response: When Ling did her best, the kids were nice to her.

Common Core State Standards

Questions 1–4: **Literature 1.** Ask and answer questions about key details in a text. **Literature 3.** Describe characters, settings, and major events in a story, using key details.

Fresh Reads Unit 4 Week 6 SI

Name _____

Read the selection. Then answer the questions that follow.

Rose's Plane Trip

Rose and Mom will take a plane trip to see Granny. | 11

Granny's home is far away. Rose is a tiny bit scared. She has | 24

never gotten on a plane before, and the plane is big! | 35

Rose and Mom wait in long lines. Nice people smile at | 46

them. Rose smiles back. Rose starts to feel better. Then it is | 58

their turn. Rose and Mom get on the plane. Rose sits by the | 71

window and stares at the ground below. Then the plane takes | 82

off, and Rose gets snacks. She likes them, and she likes the | 94

tray at her seat. Flying is fun! | 101

Turn the page.

- -

Answer the questions below.

1 **How did Rose feel at the _beginning_ of the story?**

○ very happy

● a little scared

○ hungry and sleepy

2 **Why did Rose and Mom go on the plane trip?**

● to visit Granny

○ to wait in lines

○ to eat a snack

3 **Rose did not want to fly because**

● it was her first time on a plane.

○ her mother was there with her.

○ the tray at her seat was too big.

4 **What made Rose feel better?**

○ Granny called Rose.

○ Rose sat by Mom.

● People smiled at Rose.

5 **What made Rose think it was fun to fly?**

Possible response: She liked looking out the window and having snacks.

Common Core State Standards

Questions 1–5: **Literature 1.** Ask and answer questions about key details in a text. **Literature 3.** Describe characters, settings, and major events in a story, using key details.

Name _____

Read the selection. Then answer the questions that follow.

Be Careful!

Jean hurried to get dressed. She wore her new boots with	11
the long laces. She tied the laces in big bows. Jean had to take	25
treats to school. She and Mom had made yummy popcorn	35
balls. When Jean left for school, Mom gave her a big bag of	48
popcorn balls. "Be careful," said Mom. "Do not drop the bag."	59
Jean went down the back steps. Then she tripped! Her boot	70
lace had come untied. She dropped the bag. Mom quickly	80
picked it up. Jean tightly tied her boot laces. Mom handed Jean	92
the bag again. "Be careful," she said, smiling at Jean.	102

Turn the page.

Answer the questions below.

1 **Why did Jean need to make popcorn balls?**

- ● to take a treat to school
- ○ to drop on the back steps
- ○ to eat them with Mom

2 **What made Jean trip?**

- ● Her laces came untied.
- ○ The bag fell at her feet.
- ○ Mom said to hurry up.

3 **Where did Jean trip?**

- ○ at her school
- ● on the steps
- ○ at the park

4 **Why did Mom tell Jean to be careful?**

Possible response: Mom wanted Jean to hang on to the bag.

5 **Why did Jean tie her boot laces tightly at the *end*?**

Possible response: Jean did not want to trip again.

Common Core State Standards

Questions 1–5: Literature 1. Ask and answer questions about key details in a text. **Literature 3.** Describe characters, settings, and major events in a story, using key details.

Copyright © Pearson Education, Inc., or its affiliates. All Rights Reserved.

Fresh Reads   Unit 4 Week 6 A

Read the selection. Then answer the questions that follow.

Hope and the Snake

Hope went to the well for water every day. She carried a	12
bucket to the well and back to her home. She followed the	24
same path every day. One day she met a snake on the path.	37
Hope acted brave. She stopped and stayed very still. She	47
waited. The snake passed, and Hope went on home.	56

Turn the page.

Answer the questions below.

1 **What is Hope like?**

- ● brave
- ○ silly
- ○ funny

2 **Where does Hope stand and wait?**

- ○ in her house
- ● on the path
- ○ in the water

3 **What happens at the *end* of the story?**

- ● Hope walks home.
- ○ Hope sees a snake.
- ○ Hope stops at the well.

4 **What is the big idea in this story?**

Possible response: Hope is brave when she meets a snake.

Common Core State Standards

Questions 1–4: Literature 2. Retell stories, including key details, and demonstrate understanding of their central message or lesson. **Literature 3.** Describe characters, settings, and major events in a story, using key details.

Name _____

Read the selection. Then answer the questions that follow.

Henry's Train Set

Henry had a train set with bright red train cars. The cars	12
ran on a set of black train tracks. Henry set up the train in	26
his room. He laid the tracks in the shape of an egg. The train	40
tracks went under hills and ran by creeks.	48
Henry had fun running his train around the tracks. Henry	58
had a little sister named Mary. She asked to play with the train.	71
"You are too small to know how to run the train," said	83
Henry.	84
Mary said, "You just do not want to share."	93
Henry said, "You are right. I am sorry. We can play with	105
the train together."	108

Turn the page.

Answer the questions below.

1 **What happens at the *beginning* of the story?**

- ● Henry sets up his train set in his room.
- ○ Mary wants to play with the train.
- ○ Henry asks Mary to play with him.

2 **How do you think Mary feels at the *end* of the story?**

- ○ too little to play with trains
- ● happy that she spoke up
- ○ afraid of Henry

3 **Where does this story take place?**

- ○ in the yard
- ○ at Mary's school
- ● in Henry's room

4 **What happens at the *end* of the story?**

- ○ Henry tells Mary to go away.
- ● Henry asks Mary to play.
- ○ Henry sets up the train tracks.

5 **What is the big idea of this story?**

Henry learns to share his toy.

Common Core State Standards

Questions 1–5: Literature 2. Retell stories, including key details, and demonstrate understanding of their central message or lesson. Literature 3. Describe characters, settings, and major events in a story, using key details.

Name _____

Read the selection. Then answer the questions that follow.

Big Things

Jed liked big things. He liked big dogs and big cats. He	12
liked big parties and big fun. Jed wished he was bigger!	23
"When will I get big?" he asked Dad. "I want to be big and	37
tall."	38
Dad said, "You will get big when you grow more. You will	50
get big at the right time."	56
Jed was not happy. He wanted to be big now. He went out	69
and hung by his hands for a long time on a tree branch. Maybe	83
that would help him get taller faster. But when he went inside,	95
he was still the same size.	101
"I think I will just have to wait to get bigger," said Jed.	114

Turn the page.

Answer the questions below.

1 **Where is Jed at the *beginning* of the story?**

○ in a tree

○ in a school

● in his house

2 **How does Jed try to get bigger?**

● He hangs in a tree.

○ He eats more food.

○ He asks Dad for help.

3 **What happens at the *end* of the story?**

○ Jed gets bigger.

● Jed waits to grow up.

○ Jed grows fast.

4 **How do you think Dad feels about Jed's wish?**

Possible response: Dad thinks Jed is in a hurry to grow up.

5 **What is the big idea in this story?**

Possible response: It is hard to wait for good things to happen.

1 Copyright © Pearson Education, Inc., or its affiliates. All Rights Reserved.

Common Core State Standards

Questions 1–5: **Literature 2.** Retell stories, including key details, and demonstrate understanding of their central message or lesson. **Literature 3.** Describe characters, settings, and major events in a story, using key details.

Name _____

Read the selection. Then answer the questions that follow.

Rainy Day

Peg went to the park every day with her dog, Max. She led   13

Max to the park so he could play outside.   22

One day Peg and Max left for the park. They went down   34

the back steps. Then it started to rain hard. Max did not care   47

that it was raining. Peg got her raincoat, and off they went to   60

the park!   62

Turn the page.

Answer the questions below.

1 **What is this story all about?**

○ taking good care of your pet

● going to the park every day

○ wearing raincoats to be dry

2 **How does Peg feel when she walks with Max?**

○ sad

○ angry

● happy

3 **Why does Peg take Max with her?**

○ Max hates to play in the rain.

○ Max goes everywhere with Peg.

● Max enjoys going to the park.

4 **Why does Peg get her raincoat?**

Possible response: Peg must put it on because it is raining and she would get wet.

Common Core State Standards

Question 1: Literature 2. Retell stories, including key details, and demonstrate understanding of their central message or lesson.
Questions 2–4: Literature 1. Ask and answer questions about key details in a text. **Literature 3.** Describe characters, settings, and major events in a story, using key details.

Name _____

Read the selection. Then answer the questions that follow.

Dinner for Mom

Mark and Dad will make a chicken dinner for Mom. She	11
will be getting home from a trip. Mark and Dad hope that	23
Mom will feel loved when she gets home. She will not need to	36
make dinner for them.	40
Mark and Dad clean their hands. Mark and Dad mix up	51
a cake from a box. They bake the cake while they clean the	64
chicken. Then they put salt and pepper on the chicken. They	75
lay the chicken in a long pan. They take the cake out and then	89
bake the chicken. It starts to smell very good just in time. Here	102
is Mom!	104

Turn the page.

Answer the questions below.

1 **What is this story all about?**

○ a smell

● a dinner

○ a trip

2 **When is Mom's trip?**

○ last week

● that day

○ next month

3 **Why do Mark and Dad clean their hands?**

○ They are getting ready to eat.

○ They are getting ready for bed.

● They are getting ready to cook.

4 **Why do they put salt and pepper on the chicken?**

● to make it taste better

○ to make it cleaner

○ to make it cook faster

5 **How do you think Mom feels when she gets home?**

Possible response: She is happy and feels loved.

Common Core State Standards

Question 1: Literature 2. Retell stories, including key details, and demonstrate understanding of their central message or lesson.
Questions 2–5: Literature 1. Ask and answer questions about key details in a text. Literature 3. Describe characters, settings, and major events in a story, using key details.

Name _____

Read the selection. Then answer the questions that follow.

Find It!

Sally and Bill went on a fun hunt with some friends. It was	13
a hunt to find things. Each kid had a list of things to find. The	28
first one to bring back all the things on the list would be the	42
winner.	43
Sally wanted to win. She needed to work fast to get	54
everything on her list. First she went next door and got a	66
feather hat. Then she found a tree and got two red leaves from	79
a branch. She dug a deep hole and got a worm.	90
Sally got back first with all the things on her list. She was	103
the winner of the fun hunt!	109

Turn the page.

Answer the questions below.

1 What was on the lists?

- ⭕ things to get as presents
- ⭕ things that had been lost
- ⚫ things for them to find

2 Why did Sally go find a tree?

- ⚫ She needed two leaves.
- ⭕ She needed a branch.
- ⭕ She needed a worm.

3 What was this story all about?

- ⭕ hunting for birds
- ⚫ having a contest
- ⭕ seeing a neighborhood

4 How did they pick the winner?

Possible response: The winner was the first one to find everything.

5 What did Sally have to work the hardest to get?

Possible response: She had to dig a deep hole to find a worm.

Common Core State Standards

Questions 1, 2, 4, 5: Literature 1. Ask and answer questions about key details in a text. **Literature 3.** Describe characters, settings, and major events in a story, using key details. **Question 3: Literature 2.** Retell stories, including key details, and demonstrate understanding of their central message or lesson.

Fresh Reads Unit 5 Week 2 A

Name _____

Read the selection. Then answer the questions that follow.

The Detectives

Greg and Jill are detectives. Greg wanted to find a missing | 11

painting. Jill wanted to find a missing ring. | 19

Greg looked for the painting. He saw it in a shop. A man | 32

had the painting. He was fixing the frame. Greg smiled. The | 43

mystery was solved! | 46

Jill looked for the ring. She looked up and down. She saw | 58

the ring in the dirt. Jill smiled. The mystery was solved! | 69

Turn the page.

Answer the questions below.

1 **What is the big idea in this story?**

● It is fun to solve a mystery.

○ Kids like to make new friends.

○ People need to work together.

2 **How are Jill and Greg _alike_?**

○ They like shopping.

○ They have on rings.

● They are detectives.

3 **How is Jill _not like_ Greg?**

● She looks for a ring.

○ She looks for a painting.

○ She looks in a shop.

4 **What is something that Greg and Jill do _alike_?**

Possible response: They both solve their mystery.

Common Core State Standards

Question 1: Literature 2. Retell stories, including key details, and demonstrate understanding of their central message or lesson.
Questions 2–4: Literature 1. Ask and answer questions about key details in a text. **Literature 9.** Compare and contrast the adventures and experiences of characters in stories.

Read the selection. Then answer the questions that follow.

Two Friends

Hummingbird felt sad. She wished she could spend more	9
time with her pal Beaver. Beaver lived under a dam in the	21
stream.	22
"Beaver, will you take me for a ride on your back?" asked	34
Hummingbird. She liked to hang onto Beaver's dark fur and	44
float on the stream.	48
Beaver liked Hummingbird's light, bright feathers.	54
Hummingbird was so tiny that Beaver did not feel her sitting	65
on his back.	68
When they got out of the water, Beaver went into the	79
trees. Hummingbird stayed by his side so they could chat. Her	90
wings went so fast they hummed! They had a lot of fun, and	103
Hummingbird had a happy day after all.	110

Turn the page.

Answer the questions below.

1 **What is the big idea in this story?**

○ It is fun to ride on a stream.

● It is good to have friends.

○ It is sad to live under a dam.

2 **How are Hummingbird and Beaver the *same*?**

○ They have light feathers on their backs.

○ They live in the trees by the water.

● They like floating down the stream.

3 **How is Hummingbird *not* the same as Beaver?**

● Hummingbird can fly.

○ Hummingbird is an animal.

○ Hummingbird has fur.

4 **Hummingbird and Beaver are *alike* because both can**

○ swim.

● talk.

○ fly.

5 **What is a way that Hummingbird and Beaver are *not alike*?**

Possible response: Hummingbird

has feathers, but Beaver has fur.

Common Core State Standards

Question 1: Literature 2. Retell stories, including key details, and demonstrate understanding of their central message or lesson.
Questions 2–5: Literature 1. Ask and answer questions about key details in a text. **Literature 9.** Compare and contrast the adventures and experiences of characters in stories.

Read the selection. Then answer the questions that follow.

Squirrels

Gail is a gray squirrel. Rod is a red squirrel. Gail and Rod	13
live in trees. Gail and her family sleep in nests. Rod sleeps by	26
himself.	27
Gail and Rod like to eat. Gail eats nuts, seeds, and bugs.	39
She digs holes to store food. She eats the stored food in winter	52
when it is too icy to find seeds and bugs. Rod eats pine cones	66
and nuts. He hides them in places like stone walls so he has	79
food in winter.	82
When squirrels are afraid, they tell each other. Gail waves	92
her furry tail. Rod stamps his feet. This lets other squirrels	103
know that they are not safe.	109

Turn the page.

Answer the questions below.

1 **What is the big idea in this story?**

○ All squirrels do the very same things.

● Squirrels work hard to keep their food.

○ It is good for red squirrels to stay safe.

2 **How are Gail and Rod the *same*?**

○ They like to sleep alone.

● They store winter food.

○ They are both gray.

3 **What is one way that Gail is *not like* Rod?**

● Gail eats bugs.

○ Gail has a tail.

○ Gail lives in trees.

4 **What do Gail and Rod eat that is the *same*?**

They both eat nuts.

5 **How is Rod *not like* Gail?**

Possible response: When scared, Rod stamps his feet. But Gail waves her tail.

Common Core State Standards

Question 1: Literature 2. Retell stories, including key details, and demonstrate understanding of their central message or lesson.
Questions 2–5: Literature 1. Ask and answer questions about key details in a text. **Literature 9.** Compare and contrast the adventures and experiences of characters in stories.

Name _____

Read the selection. Then answer the questions that follow.

Noses and Hoses

Elephants have long trunks. Elephant trunks are noses,	8
but they are much more. Elephant trunks can scratch an	18
itch. Elephants fill their trunks with water and use them like	29
hoses to spray their backs. This way they stay cool and wet.	41
Elephants drink by spraying water into their mouths with their	51
trunks. Trunks can smell and feel. Trunks can be noses and	62
hoses!	63

Turn the page.

Answer the questions below.

1 **Which sentence *best* tells what this selection is all about?**

○ Elephants use their trunks to drink water.

○ An elephant's trunk can scratch an itch.

● Elephant trunks can do many things.

2 **What does an elephant use its trunk for?**

● to smell

○ to see

○ to hear

3 **What is another good name for this selection?**

○ Water Hoses

● An Elephant's Tool Kit

○ Wet Animals

4 **How is an elephant's trunk *not* the same as a person's nose?**

Answers may vary. Possible response: An elephant uses it to do many more things than smelling.

Common Core State Standards

Questions 1–4: Informational Text 1. Ask and answer questions about key details in a text. Informational Text 2. Identify the main topic and retell key details of a text.

Name _____

Read the selection. Then answer the questions that follow.

Keep Your Hands Clean!

It is not fun to get a cold. It is hard to feel good when you	16
get one. Your nose gets all stuffed up, and your head hurts. You	29
may sneeze a lot.	33
Everyone gets a cold sooner or later. Many colds happen	43
in winter, and this is bad enough. But when you get a cold in	57
summer, it is very bad! The sun is shining brightly, and you	69
are stuck sick in bed. It is not fair! Drink lots of water, and get	84
plenty of rest. You will feel better soon.	92
The best thing is to not get a cold in the first place. The	106
best way to keep from getting a cold is to keep your hands	119
very clean with lots of soap and water.	127

Turn the page.

Answer the questions below.

1 This selection is *mostly* about how to handle

- ○ winter.
- ● colds.
- ○ soap.

2 What is this selection all about?

- ● dealing with getting a cold
- ○ being inside in the summer
- ○ playing outside in the sun

3 What do you need to do if you have a cold?

- ● Drink lots of water.
- ○ Play in the sun.
- ○ Go to school.

4 What is the *best* way to keep from getting a cold?

- ○ Stay in your home.
- ○ Blow your nose.
- ● Wash your hands.

5 Why is it harder to have a cold in the summer than in the winter?

Possible response: You have to be inside while it is warm and sunny outside.

⌐ **Common Core State Standards**

Questions 1–5: Informational Text 1. Ask and answer questions about key details in a text. **Informational Text 2.** Identify the main topic and retell key details of a text.

Name _____

Read the selection. Then answer the questions that follow.

How Skunks Stay Safe

Skunks have a spray called musk that smells very bad.	10
Skunks spray musk to chase away enemies. Skunks spray	19
when they are scared.	23
Skunks give warnings before they spray. They stamp their	32
feet and growl. If the threat comes closer, the skunk raises its	44
tail. The tail's white tip still hangs down. If the skunk's enemy	56
takes one more step, that tip goes up. This is bad news for	69
the enemy! The skunk shoots two jets of spray. It stinks! The	81
enemy runs away fast.	85
One animal is not scared of the skunk's spray. The Great	96
Horned Owl likes to eat skunks. The owls swoop down on	107
skunks and catch them before they can spray. This is the way	119
they beat skunks.	122

Turn the page.

Answer the questions below.

1 **What is this selection all about?**

○ a dance to scare owls

○ a white tail to catch mice

● a spray to keep enemies away

2 **What is skunk spray called?**

● musk

○ jets

○ feet

3 **How many jets of spray does a skunk shoot at its enemy?**

○ one

● two

○ three

4 **What would be another good name for this selection?**

Answers may vary. Possible response: A Smelly Surprise

5 **How are the owls *not* the same as other enemies of the skunk?**

Possible response: Owls are not stopped by the skunk's musk.

Common Core State Standards

Questions 1–5: **Informational Text 1.** Ask and answer questions about key details in a text. **Informational Text 2.** Identify the main topic and retell key details of a text.

Name _____

Read the selection. Then answer the questions that follow.

Boy and Frog

A boy sat on a log by a pond. He was having fun fishing by | 15

himself when he heard a voice. | 21

The voice was a frog saying, "Hi, Boy. May I speak with | 33

you?" | 34

"Not right now," said Boy. | 39

"But I can grant you a wish," said Frog. | 48

"Then I wish you would just let me catch fish by myself!" | 60

said Boy. | 62

Turn the page.

Answer the questions below.

1 **What happens *first* in the story?**

○ A boy hears a frog.

○ A boy gets a wish.

● A boy sits on a log.

2 **What happens *next* in the story?**

○ The boy catches a fish.

● A frog talks to the boy.

○ A frog makes a wish.

3 **What wish must the frog grant?**

● He must let the boy catch fish.

○ He must play catch with the boy.

○ He must catch up with the boy.

4 **What happens *last* in the story?**

Possible response: The boy makes a wish.

Common Core State Standards

Questions 1–4: Literature 1. Ask and answer questions about key details in a text. **Literature 3.** Describe characters, settings, and major events in a story, using key details.

Read the selection. Then answer the questions that follow.

Snow Surprise

Jen woke up one day and saw that lots of snow had fallen.	13
She just sat in bed and looked out her window at it all.	26
Then she called out, "School must be closed today!" No	36
one called back to her. Jen got up and dressed.	46
"Mom? Dad? Is school closed today?" asked Jen. There	55
was still no sound. Then Jen looked outside the back door. She	67
saw Mom and Dad playing in the snow. They were making	79
a big, fat snowman! Why weren't they getting ready to go to	89
work?	96
"Hi!" Jen called. "What are you doing?"	106
Mom just smiled and tossed a snowball at Dad. Jen put on	117
her coat and mittens. She would help them with that snowman!	120

Turn the page.

Answer the questions below.

1 **What happens *first* in the story?**

○ Mom throws a snowball.

○ Jen gets dressed.

● A lot of snow falls.

2 **What happens *after* Jen calls out?**

● Jen hears nothing.

○ Jen wakes up.

○ Jen sees snow.

3 **What happens in the *middle* of the story?**

○ Jen sits up in bed and sees the snow.

○ Jen gets ready to go outside and play.

● Jen sees Mom and Dad in the snow.

4 **What does Jen do *after* she sees Mom toss a snowball?**

○ She gets out of bed.

○ She looks out the door.

● She puts on her coat.

5 **Why does Jen feel happy?**

Possible response: It is snowing, and she does not have school.

Common Core State Standards

Questions 1–5: Literature 1. Ask and answer questions about key details in a text. **Literature 3.** Describe characters, settings, and major events in a story, using key details.

Name _____

Read the selection. Then answer the questions that follow.

Mother's Day

Tim had big plans for Mom on Mother's Day. He would | 11

do nice things for her to show her how much he cared for her. | 25

He got up and ran the vacuum cleaner. It slipped out of Tim's | 38

hands and hit the wall. It left a small hole, but Tim thought he | 52

could fix it. Then he made eggs and toast for Mom. The eggs | 65

stuck to the pan and got burned. Then Tim mowed the grass, | 77

but he ran over Mom's flowers. | 83

Mom said that Tim gave her much more than she needed. | 94

She also said that she loved him for trying to make her | 106

Mother's Day a good one. Tim said he would help Mom clean | 118

up all her surprises! | 122

Turn the page.

Answer the questions below.

1 **What happened _first_ in this story?**

- ● Tim made big plans.
- ○ Tim surprised Mom.
- ○ Tim mowed the lawn.

2 **What happened right _after_ Tim got up?**

- ○ Tim made some eggs.
- ● Tim vacuumed the rug.
- ○ Tim burned the flowers.

3 **Why did Tim want to surprise his Mom?**

- ○ It was Mom's birthday.
- ● It was Mother's Day.
- ○ Mom had been sick.

4 **What happened _after_ the lawn got mowed?**

Possible response: Mom was
surprised.

5 **What happened _last_?**

Possible response: Tim offered
to help Mom clean up.

⌐ **Common Core State Standards**

Questions 1–5: Literature 1. Ask and answer questions about key details in a text. **Literature 3.** Describe characters, settings, and major events in a story, using key details.

Name _____

Read the selection. Then answer the questions that follow.

The New Baby

Mom and Dad think Cindy's baby brother is very cute.	10
Cindy isn't sure. She thinks he may be a little bit cute. But he	23
seems to cry so much. When he is sleeping, no one can shout	36
or sing or talk in the house. Cindy loves him very much. But	48
some days she wants to be an only child again!	60

Turn the page.

- -

Answer the questions below.

1 **What does Cindy learn in the story?**

- ● She loves her brother.
- ○ She likes all babies.
- ○ She is a good sister.

2 **What is the big idea in this story?**

- ○ Babies are always fun to have around.
- ○ All babies are cute.
- ● Being a big sister can be hard at first.

3 **What did you learn about people from this story?**

- ● Family changes are sometimes hard to handle.
- ○ Sharing toys with others is always easy.
- ○ Friendship is a very good thing.

4 **What happens at the *end* of this story?**

Possible response: Cindy wishes she is still an only child.

1 Copyright © Pearson Education, Inc., or its affiliates. All Rights Reserved.

Common Core State Standards

Questions 1–4: Literature 2. Retell stories, including key details, and demonstrate understanding of their central message or lesson. **Literature 3.** Describe characters, settings, and major events in a story, using key details.

Name _____

Read the selection. Then answer the questions that follow.

Plenty for All

Rabbit came to the water hole to get a drink. Frog and	12
Turtle sat by the dry hole.	18
"We can not drink," said Frog. "We are out of water!"	29
Turtle asked, "What will we do?"	35
Rabbit said, "We can dig down. We will find water when	46
we make the hole deeper and bigger."	53
So Rabbit and Turtle started digging. It was hot, hard work.	64
But then cool water began to bubble up in the hole. Soon there	77
was plenty of water for all.	83
Rabbit said, "Frog did not help us dig. He may not take a	96
drink of our water."	100
"That is silly," said Turtle. "Be kind! If Frog gets no water,	112
he will get sick. His skin will dry out."	121
Rabbit said, "You are right. It is best to share with all of	134
us."	135

Turn the page.

Answer the questions below.

1 **What happens at the *beginning* of this story?**

○ Animals dig to find water.

● Animals come to drink water.

○ Animals find cool water.

2 **What is the big idea in this story?**

● learning to share

○ digging a hole

○ having some food

3 **What did you learn about friendship from this story?**

○ It is not right to share.

● Be kind to others.

○ Listen to the turtles.

4 **What would be another good name for this story?**

○ Rabbit Changes His Mind

● Sharing with Others

○ Frog Digs a Hole

5 **What does Rabbit learn from the story?**

Possible response: Rabbit learns that Turtle is right about sharing.

Copyright © Pearson Education, Inc., or its affiliates. All Rights Reserved.

Common Core State Standards

Questions 1–5: Literature 2. Retell stories, including key details, and demonstrate understanding of their central message or lesson. **Literature 3.** Describe characters, settings, and major events in a story, using key details.

214

Fresh Reads   Unit 5 Week 6 OL

Name _____

Read the selection. Then answer the questions that follow.

Making a New Machine

Tom hoped to be an inventor. He entered a contest for	11
children who wanted to make new things that nobody had ever	22
seen before. Tom decided to make a machine to help children	33
learn to play the piano.	38
Tom worked on his new machine. He made a piano that lit	50
up when a child played it. The light blinked to show children	62
where to put their fingers to play a song. The lights had to go	76
on and off just right for each song. It was hard work!	88
At first Tom did not get the machine to work right. But he	101
kept trying. He learned from his mistakes. At last he found	112
out how to make it work. He made the perfect piano to teach	125
children, and he got first prize!	131

Turn the page.

Answer the questions below.

1 **What is the big idea in this story?**

- ○ Do not tell lies.
- ● Keep on trying.
- ○ Remember old friends.

2 **What did you learn about Tom from this story?**

- ○ He likes to play guitar.
- ○ He does not like hard work.
- ● He does not give up.

3 **What does Tom learn in the story?**

- ● to use a mistake to do better
- ○ to stop inventing anything
- ○ to throw away things that do not work

4 **What happened to Tom at the *end* of the story?**

He won first prize in the

contest.

5 **What is another good title for this story?**

Possible response: Learn from

Your Mistakes

Common Core State Standards

Questions 1–5: **Literature 2.** Retell stories, including key details, and demonstrate understanding of their central message or lesson. **Literature 3.** Describe characters, settings, and major events in a story, using key details.